How to Succeed as a Solo Consultant

How to Succeed as a Solo Consultant

Breaking Out on Your Own

Stephen D. Field

BEP BUSINESS EXPERT PRESS

How to Succeed as a Solo Consultant: Breaking Out on Your Own

Copyright © Business Expert Press, LLC, 2020.

Cover image licensed by Ingram Image, StockPhotoSecrets.com

First published in 2020 by
Business Expert Press, LLC
222 East 46th Street, New York, NY 10017
www.businessexpertpress.com

ISBN-13: 978-1-95152-716-7 (paperback)
ISBN-13: 978-1-95152-717-4 (e-book)

Business Expert Press Entrepreneurship and Small Business Management Collection

Collection ISSN: 1946-5653 (print)
Collection ISSN: 1946-5661 (electronic)

Cover and interior design by Exeter Premedia Services Private Ltd., Chennai, India

First edition: 2020

10 9 8 7 6 5 4 3 2 1

Printed in the United States of America.

Testimonials

If you have thought of being a consultant, this book is an extremely valuable blueprint for making it a reality. It is one of the most practical books I have ever had the pleasure of reading and absorbing on this topic. Based on his years of experience as a successful business consultant, Stephen shows you what you need to know and do to become a success in this difficult and sometimes perplexing career. A must read for those starting out and/or already practicing.

—Tom Borg, Founder and President, Tom Borg Consulting, LLC

I have been helping connect people with their dream careers for over a decade, and have had a front row seat to the changing workplace and talent market. The advice in this book will help anyone prepare to make the leap into consulting and will give them the confidence and tools to succeed. I wish I had this book as a resource when I launched my consulting practice!

—Amy Cell, Chief Matchmaker, Amy Cell Talent

Stephen's book is a must read for anyone in the consulting business, or for anyone thinking of starting a consulting practice. It is well thought out, very thorough, comprehensive, and includes lots of great resources. Stephen's experience as a Consultant is invaluable, and gives the reader many insights into the real world of what it takes to be a successful consultant while maintaining a good work/life balance. Resources include templates, logs, agreements, and contracts: All essential tools for professional consultants.

—Brian Bunderson, Chief Encouragement Officer, Ann Arbor Connectors Club

Abstract

This book is written for the person who has gained workplace or other experience and is thinking about striking out on his or her own as a consultant or a service-based entrepreneur. The reader will be walked through the steps of deciding on whether they have the tools to start a new business and what they need to do before making the leap. The author focuses on the major steps of a start-up consulting practice, including business formation decisions, verbalizing the business offerings, determining market viability, setting billable rates, and marketing, selling, and delivering services. Additionally, he dives into less-often discussed topics such as office space, business insurance, business ethics, and the impact on the family unit. Each chapter provides homework that outlines the steps the reader needs to complete to gain confidence they have the tools to succeed. The book appendices include sample contracts and other useful templates.

This book also emphasizes the lifestyle implications for any lone professional. While the main focus of this book is on consulting, many of the points are applicable to a solo practitioner in any service profession.

Keywords

consulting; becoming a consultant; business startup; consultant; consulting prerequisites; lifestyle business; networking; pricing services; selling services; solopreneur; starting business; starting consulting business; working for yourself; business formation; business ethics; work family dynamics

Contents

Preface

Have you ever thought about having your own business? Not one trying to become the next Amazon, but one where you are the sole owner with no employees and no obligations to others outside your immediate family. You get to choose the services you provide. You find the clients and you perform the work. You set the schedule for when you work and, importantly, when you enjoy other leisure activities. If your answer is yes, this book was written for you.

Two-thirds of my career have been spent as a consultant. I received help and guidance from many individuals along the way; this book is my attempt to pass knowledge along to others. Starting a business is hard, and knowing where some land mines are buried will hopefully help you along on the journey.

I graduated from business school back in the late 1970s when America was still unquestionably number one and the Big 3 ruled the auto industry. For my fellow graduates, consulting was one of the most desirable and lucrative industries to join. I am not sure any of us really understood what it meant to be a consultant (other than big earnings potential), but many were ready to take a crack at it. The consulting profession had a particular mystique about it and selected only the brightest or most well-connected individuals.

I did not end up in a consulting firm. In fact, I never really considered consulting at that time. I was more interested in operations management. During my career, I had the opportunity to work with a number of different consultants, some better than others. Many consultants considered themselves the smartest person in the room, bringing expertise that could not be fathomed by the rest of us mere mortals. The truth of the matter is much simpler: good consultants bring to the table a skill set their customers need to resolve a specific issue or problem. The issue may be something that can be solved very quickly or one that stretches out for years (particularly if the client has no desire to learn the skills internally).

Anyone who has been around or worked with consultants has had the passing thought, "Hey, I can do that!" And perhaps, you can. Large consulting firms are always looking for new talent. But there is another option: starting your own consulting practice. This is an important decision and will impact your lifestyle in ways you can hardly imagine. It took me almost 20 years and a kick in the butt, before I was ready. Maybe *you* are finally ready to break out on your own.

This book also focuses on the lifestyle implications of a service-based business model. That would be any business where owners are selling their mental expertise or services (e.g., design work, problem-solving, consulting) rather than their manual dexterity (e.g., massage therapist, home remodeler) or providing products (e.g., home crafts, cosmetics).

Large consulting firms hire college graduates by the thousands and train them to be consultants, but this book is written for the person already out in the working world who has gained workplace experience and is thinking about striking out on his or her own as a consultant or similar service-based entrepreneur.

Regardless of whether you are a high-school dropout, a recent college graduate, or someone who has been in the workforce for 20+ years, I strongly advise you read at least Chapter 2 of this book before starting your own consulting practice. While the main focus of this book is on consulting, many of the points are applicable to a sole practitioner in any service profession or, for that matter, any lifestyle business.

Some readers may already have a lucrative, if not totally rewarding, day job. Before turning in your resignation letter, work through the homework assignments in each chapter to make sure you are truly prepared to embark on a consulting career. This is not an Indiana Jones leap of faith moment. You need to be sufficiently prepared and have a well-documented plan. In a best-case scenario, you might even be able to launch your consulting business before leaving the security blanket of a normal job.

In preparing to write this book, I interviewed other consultants who chose the lifestyle route and have included many of their thoughts as well as my own. I received invaluable help and guidance from Mike Diaz, Paul Larned, David Murray, and Greg Peters. I truly thank them for their input, and hope this book helps anyone thinking about becoming a consultant better understand the gains and sacrifices that come with that decision.

****

This book highlights my experiences and those of others I have encountered. It is not intended to provide professional legal or accounting advice which varies state to state.

CHAPTER 1

Solopreneur Consulting

There comes a time when you ought to start doing what you want. I think you are out of your mind if you keep taking jobs that you don't like because you think it will look good on your resume. Isn't that a little like saving up sex for your old age?

—Warren Buffett

Con-sul'-tant: An experienced professional with wide knowledge in a specific field who provides expert advice or services in a particular area to a business or individual.

Anyone can call himself or herself a consultant. There is no legal protection given to the job title. There is no industry regulation, training, or certification process, as is the case for doctors, architects, or even realtors. But you do not just want the title of consultant; you want to be a successful consultant.

Here are four characteristics that distinguish a consultant from other professions:

- Consultants provide expertise that clients lack. This can be an unfilled opening at a company or simply the need to add skill capacity for a certain period of time. Consultants hold a knowledge advantage over their client.
- Consultants charge a fee for their professional services. If you are doing this for free, you are a volunteer, not a consultant.
- A consultant operates independently from the client; there can be no conflict of interests between the client's issues and the services provided. This independence can be a sticky point with the Internal Revenue Service (IRS), if not properly documented.

- A consultant operates in a professional manner, ensuring high-quality service delivery. This includes having the ability to provide the needed services and not just faking it.

This book focuses on what a *solopreneur* needs to do to successfully launch and operate a consulting *business* in order to generate the income their family needs to live in the *style they desire*.

Solopreneur reflects a start-up business consisting of only the founder. Businesses with employees create a certain level of responsibility, limiting one's flexibility. When a solopreneur service business owner retires, the business typically folds because it has minimal real business assets or any employees to carry on business activities. It is not a sustaining entity. If you have the entrepreneurial drive and energy to start a business, hire employees, and set a goal of growing it to some much larger scale, I applaud you. You will likely need to make sacrifices in your personal life for the sake of the business. That is a different path than the one described in this book. Some people are fortunate enough to travel both paths (sometimes more than once!) during their working career.

An important element of focus is on the *business*. This is not a hobby or an after-work activity. This is a full-time commitment to forming a true business entity with all of the required paperwork and operational action items. This includes dedicating the necessary time to turn the business into a functioning company.

Style they desire is the final important element. Some people get by with a very modest income, while others need more substantial resources to maintain or achieve the style of living they seek. A solopreneur consulting practice can be considered successful if it brings in adequate income for the owner and his or her family to live on (including money from other sources such as spousal earnings) and provides the flexibility for the business principal and family to enjoy their free time and achieve any other goals they have set.

Anyone can start a consultancy, but success is not guaranteed. Beginning a consulting business is the same as any other start-up company. It takes hard work and some luck. Various publications report that while more than half of all Americans of working age thought they were capable of starting their own company, only nine percent actually took the plunge and began the process.

Nevertheless, a small business owner has lots of company. There are approximately 543,000 new businesses (of every type) started each month.[1] Data from *Forbes* shows there over 24 million one-person small business operations in the United States with no payroll or employees.[2] These numbers continue to grow every year, and 52 percent of all small businesses are home-based.

Service-oriented businesses have a high dropout rate. Less than half of them survive five years.[3] Every business owner is different, and a variety of reasons explain the demise of small businesses. Do not be discouraged by this. Perhaps, your business does not need to last for five years or is merged with another. The key is to understand what you are trying to accomplish, what steps you need to take to make it happen, and what contingency plans to have in place to manage the inevitable potholes you encounter.

A business can sell services, products, or some combination of the two. Service-based companies (such as consultancies) are selling the time and expertise of the business owner. The revenue from a service-based consulting business is contingent on the total amount of time put into the business by the individual. Money remaining after expenses provides the income an individual receives. During any period of time when there is no revenue, there is no income.

Product-based companies face additional issues, including buying (financing) the raw or finished goods inventory, maintaining equipment, storing material, and shipping to customers. Unless you are independently wealthy, keep any initial inventory investment to a minimum.

---

[1] https://learn.g2.com/small-business-statistics
[2] https://forbes.com/sites/elainepofeldt/2017/05/25/new-data-more-americans-are-creating-million-dollar-one-person-businesses/#3ee5cf2b6239
[3] https://smallbiztrends.com/2012/09/failure-rates-by-sector-the-real-numbers.html

Reasons for Starting a Lifestyle Business

Gary worked for one of the Big 6 accounting firms. Terry was in brand management for packaged consumer goods. Jane worked as the art director for a medical supply company. What links these individuals and thousands of others is their decision to walk away from corporate life and start their own businesses to gain control over their lifestyle.

Some people arrive at this inflection point after having a long career, but finding themselves not ready for full retirement. Some want to volunteer their skills and knowledge to those in need. Others, mid-career, want to break out of the maze of *working for the man* and strike out on their own. Some people make this choice before ever holding any other type of job. Right out of high school or college, they start their own business. All have skills they learned over time and now want to apply those same skills to their own clients.

A growing trend among the Gen X and millennials is to no longer think of working hard for 30 years (the time of spending that with a single company is long past), climbing the corporate ladder, or playing by their parents' rules of buying a car, a house, and saving for retirement. Earlier in life, they want more control over their work/life balance. A 2016 study by Fidelity Investments found that 25- to 35-year-olds would be willing to give up $7,600 in annual pay for a healthier work/life balance.[4] (All currencies in this book are U.S. dollars.)

Many of these young people (and older brethren) are looking for opportunities today to become freelancers or entrepreneurs. Some want to have a lifestyle business allowing them to come and go as they please, to be their own boss, and to travel whenever they see fit. I encourage these people to pursue this dream as long as they have something of value to offer their customers.

Starting a solopreneur business is a choice. One does not do it out of necessity, but rather to earn a respectable income while not sacrificing the other important things in their life. Some people may want to be able to take frequent vacations. Others may desire free time to spend with a sick family member. By running a lifestyle business, I could attend my

---

[4] *Detroit Free Press*, April 17, 2016, page 4B.

children's high-school sporting events, and that was important to me. However, money not earned today cannot always be recovered in the future. Recognize the pros and cons of making this choice.

So, what kind of person do you need to be to make this career choice? Barbara Taylor of Synergy Business Services identifies three distinct types of business owners:

1. The underachiever: Business is intentionally capped or subordinated to the owner's personal life.
2. The hedonist: Business exists solely to enrich the owner and provide maximum leisure time.
3. The free spirit: Business is an expression of the owner's skills, knowledge, or passion.

Most lifestyle businesses are run by someone with a combination of the three traits; I know mine is. Do not be confused by the underachiever heading. It takes arduous work and many accomplishments to gain and maintain the flexibility to pursue other non-work interests.

Differences Working for Yourself

There are a number of important differences between working for others and working for yourself. Some of these are discussed in more detail later in this book.

The downside:

- Loss of a work community
    ◦ No more socializing around the water cooler, hearing the latest gossip
- Loss of respect in everyday life for your old position in an organization
    ◦ No longer able to delegate to underlings
- Unpredictable travel to clients (automobile, plane, or train)
    ◦ My first large consulting client involved a long difficult drive in heavy traffic several days a week. Every time I started to grumble, I would remind myself how much more

I was getting paid as a consultant and the drive became much more enjoyable.

- No more regular paychecks every two weeks or twice a month
- Your responsibility for all taxes
- Need to find the right insurance coverages—health and other
- No longer receive *paid time off* for vacations or holidays
- No overtime pay
- No one matches any contributions to your retirement account
- No annual performance reviews and salary increases
- Sole responsibility for invoicing and cash collection

The upside:

- Greater exposure to different businesses and different industries
  - My personal experience has included clients in the delicatessen business, metal stamping of automotive parts, business trade associations, life science companies, high-tech electronics, the oil and gas pipeline industry, and many others.
- Ability to pick the type of work and customers you enjoy
- Short commute to your office
  - Might just be a flight of stairs!
- Significant business decisions made by you alone
  - No longer made by committee
  - No need for higher-level approval
  - No one else to blame for bad decisions (that can also be a downside)
- New challenges, new opportunities, new rewards
- New-found respect from senior management at client companies
- Control of your earning's potential and realization

While a solopreneur business is different than typical corporate work, it is still a job, and you can be consumed by your work 24/7 if you let it. I cannot remember the last vacation I took where I did not check my e-mails or try to do some billable work activity.

A solopreneur business can be very difficult on your spouse or significant other. I will go into several family issues later in the book, but it is extremely important your spouse or significant other buys into your decision to go the lifestyle route. The impact of this choice is as significant to their lifestyle as your own and your relationship.

PART I

Do You Have What It Takes
To Be a Consultant?

CHAPTER 2

Becoming a Consultant: The Four Qualifications

The purpose of life is to live it, to taste experience to the utmost, to reach out eagerly and without fear for newer and richer experience.
—Eleanor Roosevelt

When I came out of business school, my operations management courses had consisted of one combined semester of cost accounting and linear programming. While both of these tools still have a place in the business world, my real knowledge of operations management came from on-the-job training. During my 20 plus years in manufacturing, I worked for four different companies, was responsible for maintaining multi-million-dollar inventories, ran several different production facilities, and led three major enterprise resource planning (ERP) software system selection and implementation projects. (ERP is the type of software manufacturers use for accounting, sales, inventory control, production control, and other key processes). Without that experience, the good times and particularly the bad, I would never have gained the knowledge that allowed me to become a consultant. It was very beneficial for me to have worked at different companies and witnessed the similarity and differences in business processes from company to company.

Here are the four distinct qualifications or attributes necessary to become a successful sole practitioner consultant:

1. In-depth knowledge base or skill set a customer needs or wants
2. Communication and people skills
3. The right mindset
4. Willingness to take on new tasks

Knowledge or Skill Set

After working for others for a number of years, you should have a general understanding how the business world, or your particular industry, works and the various skills and functions necessary for success. You have developed a set of skills that have made you successful in your current or previous position. These skills provide value to your employer and ideally for others as well.

As a buyer, I once made a mistake that cost the company about $100,000 in obsolete inventory. An engineering change came through on a Friday, and I did not notify the vendor until Monday. Turns out the vendor ran overtime production all weekend making unusable parts. (Later in my career, I sold off millions of dollars of obsolete inventory for repurposing, so I am at peace with the landfill gods.) The reason I am telling this story is that consultants cannot afford to make that kind of mistake. My employer was large enough to absorb the loss with minimal impact, but that is not always the case. Additionally, you may incur some professional liability with your client. Can you or your client afford to take a $100,000 loss? It is best to travel up the learning curve on someone else's money.

Knowledge has value. An old story has a plumber charging a large fee for banging on a pipe to solve a particular problem. When the building owner complained as to why he had to pay so much for someone hammering on a pipe, the plumber replied the charge was not for the banging, but for knowing which pipe to hit. You can charge for knowledge. Knowledge includes knowing others you call upon to complete a specific task as well as what you know yourself. This goes into the total value you provide to your customers.

Your skills or knowledge can be very general (e.g., project management) or very specific (e.g., tax treatment of manufacturing research and development credits), but you need to have in-depth knowledge in your area of expertise. I can design a website. I did my first (and last) one in the 1990s. I doubt you would pay me to design yours. I just do not have that in-depth knowledge—even when compared to kids still in high school! Spend some time thinking about how you would describe the specific services or toolset on which you want to build your business. If you have a great deal of difficulty in coming up with an answer, perhaps you are not quite ready to strike out on your own.

The next step is to verify that the skill or knowledge has current and future market value (knowledge of Fortran or even Cobol programming might be fascinating to learn, but will find a very limited market). Check with potential customers to see if the skill or knowledge you have identified is something they would be willing to pay for. Are there others already selling that service? That would indicate there is a market for it. It is always a good step to understand your competition. A lack of competition is not necessarily a good sign. It may indicate that there are other options available to solve your customers' problems, or that the problem is not painful enough to need a solution. The status quo can be your toughest competitor.

Periodically review and assess the services you are offering and how they can be updated to provide you with more enjoyable work, create more sales opportunities, or even provide a better rate on what you charge for your services. Evolve or die sounds harsh, but is a real risk for the solopreneur.

The list of potential skill sets and knowledge is endless, but here are some common examples:

Skills	Knowledge
• Accounting	QuickBooks setup
• Graphic design	Photoshop
• Engineering	AutoCAD
• Website design	Drupal Programming
• Strategic planning	Various tools
• Economic development	Non-profit management
• Fund raising	Grant writing
• Sales and marketing	Business connections
• Employee training	Focus area expertise
• Environmental regulations	Regulatory rules
• Project management	Project expertise

Communication and People Skills

Effective communication skills are required at the time of business startup to get your message out to potential customers (written communications) and to be able to sell your services face to face (oral communications). There are numerous ways of doing this, but it is important you present a clear and consistent message to help in the development of your own individual brand. More on that in Chapter 8 on marketing. A myriad of third-party resources can help with the development of your marketing materials.

Well-written contracts and progress reports are also important documents for various projects. One solution is to develop form documents you can use with slight modifications for each customer. This can be extended to e-mail templates that you use repeatedly and PowerPoint presentations that require only minor tweaks for different clients. At the end of this book, I have included some boilerplate agreements, which you can customize for your own purposes.

People skills are useful in negotiating a deal, but are even more important in managing a project. There are certain situations to keep in mind. Your presence may create conflict between what you bring to the table and the status quo of a business. You may be perceived as a threat to certain individuals. For that matter, you are an actual threat to someone's job if they are underperforming. This all needs to be well managed.

Part of communication is the ability to be a good listener. People want to open up to you, but might be afraid to speak poorly about their company or other employees. You need to read between the lines of what is being said and what they are trying to convey. Provide them with a way to speak *off the record*, so their comments are not tied back to them. You will find yourself talking to people at different levels of the organization. Working with companies, you can be talking to anyone from the maintenance crew or production workers up through the CFO and business owner. You need to treat them all as individuals who can help you in reaching the goals of your project. An attitude of arrogance only works against you.

When I am interviewing someone, I like to record the conversation. This allows me to focus more on the person I am talking to and minimizes the need to record on paper everything that is said. It takes more time (usually non-billable) to transcribe the recording, but for me, it has been well worth the effort. I make sure to let the person know I am the only one who will hear the recording and I stick to that rule. Digital voice recorders are available for less than $50. Spend more and you can find ones that do transcribing automatically.

It is very important to understand the mindset of the customers' key decision makers and to make sure you are keeping them informed of project activities on a regular basis. These may not always be the people you work with directly on the project, so it is important to recognize the difference and keep the decision makers in the loop.

Consulting projects fall victim to scope creep when the project expands outside of the original intent. It is critical to be on the lookout for this and to manage the expectations of your customer. In my work today, companies are looking for software systems that can accomplish certain tasks. As they get into the project, they learn about other unneeded bells and whistles the software can perform and can get distracted by these, if not kept on task.

This is a key area where on-the-job experience and knowledge help you get in front of problems and properly manage these issues.

The ability to be a good listener can also lead to more work. Several existing clients have complained about not having the proper resources or skills to complete required activities. By listening to their needs and being willing to take on new tasks, I have ended up conducting a physical inventory, filling out government compliance forms for the Affordable Healthcare Act, and pushing through the purchase of distressed industrial property in Detroit. I knew little about the latter two areas, but was willing to learn and take on the assignments.

The Right Mindset

It takes a certain personality type to become a sole practitioner consultant. An introvert will have a tough time getting out there and doing the hard selling. One needs to enjoy the *thrill of the hunt* in finding and landing a new customer. As anyone in sales can tell you, rejection is part of the game, and you need to be able to take that in stride.

You cannot take the rejection personally. This is business. It is wise to step back from time to time to see if there is a pattern to the business you are losing. Have the jobs gone to a lower-cost option? Did the work go to a higher-cost more credible source? Did the customer just not see the value in what you were offering?

I cannot tell you how many times I hear the line "we really liked your proposal, but…" I never mind losing work to a lower-cost option. I know the quality will not be as good as what I am offering and I am not going to cut my costs to compete on that basis. For every job, win or lose, check with the client to see why they made the decision that they did. This helps you learn your best attributes for landing new business and can uncover potential competitors.

You need to have a passion for the work you will be doing. It is one thing to be trapped in a job you do not like because you need the income. It is quite another to start your own business doing work you do not like. JUST <u>DO NOT</u> DO IT.

Passion is what is going to get you through the tough times. Passion is your compensation when you lose a job to a competitor. Passion is what is going to convince the customer you are the one they want to hire. Do not be afraid to let your passion show during your networking and sales presentations. It is who you are.

Also remind yourself that passion itself does not pay the bills. You need the confidence and backbone to stand up for the recommendations you are making, but be willing to modify those recommendations in the presence of additional information. You do not want to be perceived as wishy-washy, but an unbending belief that your solution is the only one does not serve you well. No one can know it all or be right all of the time. One of the aspects enjoyed most about consulting is the opportunity to learn about new businesses, processes, and solutions. Listen to your customer! They have been involved with their company and industry much longer than you.

The sole practitioner needs to be self-motivated. Every day, you need to be thinking about what you are going to accomplish that day. It is up to you to make sure you properly structure your day to achieve those tasks and minimize the interference of distractions (e.g., kids, the dog, warm weather, and so on). If you are not careful, it gets to be *quitting time*, and you realize you have accomplished nothing that day. Periods of time can pass where you are alone in your home office. You need to create a structure that works for you. A useful tool is to create a list of daily tasks to be accomplished and set deadlines for yourself. The pure need for income motivates some, while others need more of a push.

Clients' deadlines are more obvious and developed in agreement with the customers. When doing your own business development work, the deadlines become more arbitrary. In writing this book, I accomplished much more once I set a goal of a certain number of words to write each week.

Willingness to Take On New Tasks

What do you currently know about filing IRS Form Schedule C? What about starting up a limited liability company (LLC) organization? What about making collection calls to customers?

In a large organization, skill sets get separated into different functional areas. In a one-man band, you play all the instruments. It is important you can quickly pick up on many types of work you have never done before. Perhaps, even more important is the ability to identify and select good people who support your business. This can be a lawyer, an accountant, or even a good website designer.

Time is your most precious resource. Understand your core competencies and the value of your time. The concept of a solopreneur lifestyle business is to spend time on what is important to you. Understand what you want to be doing and what is necessary for you to do to be successful in your business. Think carefully before taking on large in-house projects. For example, you do not receive income for the time you spend developing your own website or marketing collateral materials. Can that time be better utilized in revenue-producing activities if you pay to outsource those tasks? Do not waste time when you can depend on others for their expertise.

So…

Do you have a marketable skill or knowledge base?

Do you communicate effectively and are you comfortable talking with strangers?

Can you work independently?

Are you willing to do all of the tasks that need to be done in a business?

If you answered *no* to *any* of these questions, you better think twice about becoming a solopreneur consultant. In all likelihood, your answer was probably more in the gray area, so here is a test.

First, write down what you think are your saleable skills and knowledge base—your area of expertise. Then, attend a local networking event. This could be a business networking event, a Meetup group, a political rally, or any other gathering of people. The type of event does not matter other than holding the potential to meet a likely customer. Go to the meeting and introduce yourself to strangers. Ask them what they do and eventually get around to asking them about challenges they face in your area of expertise. You should be able to introduce yourself to 15 to 20 different people. If none of the people you talk to shows any interest in your area of expertise, you either picked the wrong event or perhaps you need to rethink your offering.

If you find you are unable to talk to people in this type of setting, you are going to have some serious challenges down the road finding new business. An introvert will find one-on-one selling to be difficult. One trick my dad taught me was to ask people questions about themselves. People always like to talk about themselves and what they are doing. It is a safe way to get them to open up. They may respond by asking you the same question in return, so be ready with your answer!

Chapter 2: Homework

Most chapters will end with a list of tasks to be accomplished to help you decide if you are really ready and the steps to take to get a business started. So, to see if you are ready, complete the following:

- Determine if you have the necessary prerequisites to do consulting.
  o In depth knowledge or skill
  o Effective communication skills
  o The right mindset
  o Willingness to take on new tasks
- Think about how you will describe the specific set of skills or tools upon which you are building your business.
- Check with potential customers to see if they are willing to pay for those skills or tools.
- Start a notebook to capture your thoughts, plans, and information about your business.
  o Start with a list of what you think are your saleable skills and knowledge base.
- Attend a local networking group, introduce yourself to a variety of people, and give them your business introduction. Note their reaction and refine your introduction as necessary.
- Be honest with yourself in deciding if you have the skills to become a consultant.

CHAPTER 3

Starting a Consulting Business: The Three Prerequisites

In preparing for battle I've always found plans are useless, but planning is essential.

—Dwight Eisenhower

1. Business Plan

Every start-up business needing to raise money is required to create a solid business plan. A solopreneur consulting business has it easier. A banking or investor quality document is not required, but it is wise to record the answers to some very important questions. Not addressing these questions before starting your business results in wasted time and lost opportunities.

Capture in your notebook your answers to the following questions. You will find it useful to come back to this notebook periodically to review and update your answers. The homework section of each following chapter will provide additional content to add to your notebook.

- What are your lifestyle and business goals for the coming year(s)?
- How will you measure progress against your goals and business success?
- What services will you provide (Chapter 4)?
- Who are your customers (Chapter 4)?
- How will you price these services (Chapter 7)?
- How will you market and sell your services to your customers (Chapters 8, 9, and 10)?

Setting goals helps you establish what you want to accomplish in the coming year and set metrics against which you can measure your progress. Determine your annual business revenue goal and the timing of the income. If you wish to produce $72,000 of revenue a year, that means you should average $6,000 per month. If you want an annual revenue of $150,000, you need to average $12,500 per month. Where do you stand three months into your efforts? Six months? Maybe your plan is to ramp up your business revenue over the first year. Setting your goal to paper gives you a benchmark to monitor your progress. It also gives you numbers to share with your spouse and make sure you are both on the same page.

You should define your lifestyle goals for the year. It may be spending some number of hours per week with your family or visiting every ballpark in America or learning how to become a musician, and so on. As time goes by, track your progress against your goals.

SMART goals were first described by George Doran back in 1981. Search "SMART Goals" on the Internet to explore extensive in-depth descriptions, but the gist is that the goals need to be:

Specific: Focus on what you want to accomplish (e.g., income level, working hours)

Measurable: How will you quantify your accomplishments (e.g., revenue, # clients)?

Assignable: As a solopreneur, this generally falls on you.

Realistic: Do a sanity check to make sure the goal is reasonable. Are you really willing to work 100 hours per week?

Time-related: Specify when the result will be completed. By May 1, within one year, and so on.

For each goal you have, list the action items necessary to achieve that goal. For example, if your goal is to earn $72,000 in income, you might need to land six $12,000 jobs (or 24 at $3,000). Make sure you are comfortable with the numbers. Gaining one client at $72,000 may not be feasible or may be exactly your situation!

The answers do not need to be locked in stone. Mike Tyson famously once said, "Everyone has a plan, until they get punched in the mouth." You need the flexibility to *pivot* (current industry buzzword) if your plan is not proving successful.

When I first started in consulting, I joined a two-person firm whose target market was start-up companies. I was expecting to offer those clients my operational expertise and services. It turns out startups do not need that type of help. They need help raising money and do not have the funds to pay for operational assistance. That experience taught me much about finance, accounting, and the overall consulting business, but eventually I had to move on. I finally found my sweet spot by offering very specialized services to small- to mid-sized manufacturers and non-profit organizations.

Goal-setting is about being honest with yourself and your immediate family. Everyone must be on the same page to maintain family harmony while making your business succeed. If you goal is to be a stay-at-home mom or dad and only earn $10,000 a year, how realistic is that if your rent is $1,500 per month? Your goals and plan need to pass a sanity check. Understand it takes time to build a business. It is very unlikely your business starts out at capacity and target income levels. Anticipate a general ramp-up period where you build your client base and professional credibility.

2. Financial Contingency Plan

After a period of time, what happens if you are not meeting your goals? Perhaps, you can think of a good contingency plan today (or down the road) to still achieve your business objectives, but it is important to have a financial contingency plan in place if your business just does not work out the way you hoped.

If you are really lucky, you start your new career with one large client providing enough money to live on. At the other extreme is the person starting with no business income and having to scrape by for any work. What do these two individuals have in common? At some point, their business is going to go through a dry spell with little income. Big projects come to an end. Startups take time. The cashflow becomes a trickle or stops.

One of the least appreciated benefits of working full time is the regularity of a paycheck. The cash automatically appears each pay period. Once you are on your own, that stops. You only get paid if you have done work, and even then, the timing of the payments can be irregular.

This can be the biggest adjustment your family needs to make in accepting your decision to become a consultant. Your bank statement will have more peaks and more valleys. If your spouse does not understand and accept this, you are looking at some nasty arguments in the future.

To survive those down periods, it is important to have a financial contingency plan. That plan can include any severance you received if laid off from your last position. It can be your spouse's income if that covers your day-to-day needs. You cannot follow your lifestyle dream if you do not have enough money for basic living expenses (more on that in Chapter 6).

Other elements of your contingency plan are your savings and debt. If you are lucky enough to have non-retirement savings to live on while you build up your new business income, congratulations!

Your retirement savings have accumulated over the years with the purpose of using them after you stop working. DO NOT use that money to fund your business. If you do not have enough non-retirement assets to live on today, I am willing to bet you will need every retirement dollar you have squirreled away when you finally stop working. You have more options today than you will when you are 65, 70, or 75 years old.

You can ask to borrow money or at least verify money will be available if you need it in the future. Many start-up companies need cash and the advice is to start with the three *Fs*—family, friends, and fools. You are starting a business for your own personal lifestyle. This is not going to provide a large return for *investors* in your business. At best, they can expect their money back, perhaps with a little interest, but that is all.

It is strongly recommended you formalize any loan agreement on paper to avoid future confusion. Family and friends should not loan you any money they cannot afford to lose. You have the best intentions today, but many families and friendships have split up over money.

As far as more formal loans, banks are not going to lend you money for you to enjoy a certain lifestyle. Collateral would be required and most likely result in a second mortgage or a home equity loan. Avoid this option at the start. Maybe, after you have been in business for five years and experienced the ups and downs, you can reconsider this option, if necessary.

The final source of money to be discussed here is credit cards. Many very successful businesses started on credit card debt. If you have a good credit rating, you can actually use your credit cards to borrow money at a relatively low rate.

I want to emphasize the plural in credit cards. By accepting the best deals from the plethora of new cards I received daily in the mail (some offered $0 down, zero percent interest for xx months), I was able to transfer balances from one card to another, maintaining a low five-digit balance for several years while not incurring exorbitant interest fees. You need to make sure you pay the minimum balance every month and keep track of when the promotion ends. This only works if your credit score is already in very good shape and you can keep it there. If not, credit card interest rates are exorbitant. If you are already buried in credit card debt, starting a lifestyle business is probably not your best option.

3. A Mentor

On my first job out of business school, I was assigned to a large project and provided with a mentor. He was an older German gentleman (I often wondered how he spent his time during the Second World War) who had been with the company for many years. He was very precise on how things should be done and knew manufacturing inside and out. He made me re-staple documents if the staples were not put in vertically—never diagonally or horizontally. I was still wet behind my proverbial ears, and he was instrumental in bringing me up the learning curve.

In my first venture into consulting, I was fortunate to join forces with a person who had been in the consulting business for several years. His focus was on helping companies put together business plans and managing their finances. I think he envisioned me taking over the business someday and was very helpful in coaching me on a number of financial issues, including payroll taxes and budgeting. This was totally outside my previous areas of expertise, and I would have never gained the knowledge I received without his tutelage.

Both situations highlight several positive benefits of having a mentor. That person can greatly accelerate your learning process, provide objective feedback, and help you discover solutions to your problems based on their own experience. This does not happen right away. You need to dedicate the time to develop the right relationship with your mentor. You want to make sure you are using their time wisely. Be prepared when it is time to meet with them and have a set agenda.

It is not an absolute requirement to have a mentor before starting a business, but it can save you an enormous amount of time, money, and frustration. Even though you are striking out on your own, it is wonderful to have someone with relevant experience to talk to, bounce ideas off, and discuss unexpected problems.

You should always be talking to your spouse about the business, but he or she might not have the background to understand what you are facing or be able to help with particular issues.

A mentor does not need to be a single person. Depending on the scope and complexity of your services, you may even benefit by having more than one mentor. Numerous networking groups can fulfill this purpose. Make sure you find a group that provides the right kind of feedback, rather than pressing you for sales referrals for others in the group (those types of groups can be useful, but not as a mentoring function).

Mentors can be friends, old business colleagues, and even other consultants with different expertise. Think of this person (people) as your board of advisors; someone from whom you can seek advice, someone to present with your goals and action items, someone to provide a sanity check for some of the screwball ideas you might think up. Having a mentor provides an objective perspective, helps with development of your strategic plans, and assists in seeing the bigger picture when you get too tied up in the minutia of running a business.

The mentor can play the role of accountability partner. This is someone who helps you keep your commitments. They are your coach to assist you with those commitments. They become a trusted partner providing guidance and motivation. If you plan on making five cold calls each week, that person follows up with you to make sure that is happening and works with you through any stumbling blocks preventing that action. Having a good mentor also alleviates the you-against-the-world feelings. Someone has your back. You are not entirely on your own.

If you are fortunate, this person does not need any compensation beyond an occasional beer or perhaps a steak dinner to celebrate a particular success. Some people provide this kind of work for a living and will charge you, but their advice may be well worth it.

A good mentor should have the desire or interest to help you and to learn about your business. Make sure the person has a decent track record and current industry knowledge. You may find that you need to change or add mentors over time as your specific needs evolve.

And finally, if the mentoring relationship is not working, thank the person and cut loose. Your time is precious, and you do not need to waste it *trying to make the relationship work*. Based on what you learn after working with one person, you should be better positioned to select a mentor for the areas where you need the most assistance.

Chapter 3: Homework
Update your notebook with the following sections:
- Goals for the coming year
  - o Include your annual business revenue and estimated timing
  - o Include your lifestyle goals
- Action items necessary to achieve those goals
- Ways to measure your progress against these goals
- List of services you plan to provide
- A narrative about your customer (more in Chapter 4)
- Plans to determine the pricing model for your services (more in Chapter 7)
- Plans to market and sell your services (more in Chapters 8, 9, and 10)
- Develop a financial contingency plan
- Identify potential mentors

CHAPTER 4

Understanding Your Business Offering

Vision without execution is hallucination.

—Thomas Edison

Vision without action is a daydream. Action without vision is a nightmare.

—Japanese Proverb

From the two-person consulting firm, I moved to a larger quasi-government consulting organization where I headed up the materials management and IT practices we provided to small and mid-sized manufacturers. While I had more opportunities to work with companies on their ERP (business management software) projects, the overall focus of the firm steadily drifted away from my specialty area toward quality systems and lean manufacturing. I also got pulled into some strange situations. Anyone remember the Y2K tools consultants were offering to keep the world from ending? Yep, that was me.

Finally, I went off on my own with a more focused approach to the services I wanted to be offering. I had learned what companies needed and how I could help them.

Fortune magazine had an article (September 25, 2014) titled *Why startups fail according to their founders*.[1] The top five reasons were (my comments in italics):

1. No market need (cited by 42 percent of polled startups)

---

[1] https://fortune.com/2014/09/25/why-startups-fail-according-to-their-founders/

As mentioned earlier it is critical to be offering a service enough customers are willing to pay for. Creating a new market need can be done (e.g., Apple with the iPod, iPhone…), but that is extremely challenging and difficult for one person to do. Make sure your service offering will be desirable to your customers.

2. Shortage of cash

You are no longer receiving a regular paycheck. You need to understand how money flows into and out of your business. Do not forget about that financial contingency plan mentioned in the previous chapter.

3. Not the right team

You are the team. Either you can do this or not. If not, it is best to find out early and cut your losses. The outcompeted reason is tied into you as the team. The service you offer will not be unique. How hard is it to differentiate yourself from the other guy (whose initials could be IBM)?

4. No competitive edge

This gets back to earlier points on having the right mindset. This becomes you against the world. You need the perseverance and self-motivation to make it happen. The marketplace is full of bigger and better financed competitors, but you have many advantages they do not. You call all the shots. You make the decisions. You determine how hard you work to win a contract.

5. Pricing and cost issues

Getting the price right is important for your business. Undercharge and you will have a hard time putting in enough hours to make a decent living. Overcharge and you might lose work to the competition. Pricing will be discussed further in Chapter 7.

Now back to your services…

Paraphrasing Jim Rohn, an entrepreneur and motivational speaker, "We get paid for bringing value to the marketplace; you don't get paid for time, you get paid for value." You need to identify a service that provides value to a customer. You may be billing your customer by the hour, but what they are buying is results, not time.

Start-up companies can get all hung up on the wiz-bang features of their new product without thinking about the value to the customer. For many service businesses (and non-profits), one of the biggest challenges is identifying a value proposition. Make sure you think about this from the customer's perspective. How would you justify paying money to receive whatever service it is you plan to offer? Will it reduce costs? Will it increase sales? No matter how brilliant you think your offering, if the customer does not see the value, you will not succeed.

Mr. Rohn also said "Time is more valuable than money. You can get more money, but you cannot get more time." This important truism is the reason many people choose a lifestyle business.

Your services are a combination of your knowledge and skill sets. Knowledge is the cumulation of the theoretical information you have learned (and not forgotten) in life. Skill sets relate to how you use that knowledge to solve problems and complete tasks. Knowledge is wasted if you cannot properly apply it to a situation.

This is one of the reasons very intelligent people get tripped up when faced with an unfamiliar issue. They do not have the skill set to apply their knowledge properly.

I went skydiving once. The morning session was spent on the ground understanding how to exit the plane, deploy the parachutes, steering, landing, and what to do if there was a problem. In the afternoon, we finally took our jump. My problem was that once in the air, I had no frame of reference. I was steering the chute, but could not tell how far I was turning or moving. Fortunately, I missed landing in the parking lot. Others in my group were not as lucky, including one friend who went into the trees, but was not injured. Classroom theory alone is not enough to accurately land a parachute. Consulting based only on theory will be equally challenging.

You want to find a service that fits your skill set, and that you enjoy doing. There is no reason to be unhappy with the type of work you perform. You want to avoid becoming a *consulting whore*, willing to do any type of work for money. You need a focus to the services you offer. Without focus, marketing and selling become very difficult and costly. I suggest starting with a service that is simple to explain, and for the customer, easy to see the value. The breadth of your focus can grow as you gain more experience.

Talk to people you work with currently or in the past to get their impressions of your strengths and weaknesses. You really want to avoid setting up shop selling your weaknesses, even if you enjoy those tasks.

One good verification step at this point is to use Google AdWords to see how your services rank. You can get started on their website for free. You may find there is high demand for the keywords you would use, but that might mean there is a lot of competition for those services. (If you actually decide to use AdWords, make sure you give careful thought to the website landing page for anyone clicking on your ad.)

Another suggestion is to look for a service with follow-up work. For product companies, this is referred to as the razor blade model: customers first buy the razor, then they come back continuously to buy the replacement blades.

My consulting sweet spot is helping companies select new ERP systems (business management software). Doing my job well means my customer is buying a system they will not need to replace for 10 to 15 years. That is a long wait for repeat business! By adding an audit component to my offering, I get back in their door on a more regular basis.

See if you can describe your service offering in 25 words or less. This is only a few sentences but should be enough to gain the interest of a prospect you meet at a networking event. Some services may be so technical or complicated that a lay person would never be able to understand a 25-word description. That is okay. They are probably not your potential customer. For them you can use a more generic description. I tell those people I help companies with their front office business computer systems.

Active Versus Passive Offerings

Selling your time to perform a service produces active income. Your actions require time to create the value that allows you to bill a customer. Regardless of whether you are welding metal, doing market research, or studying plant floor operations, you are spending your own time in performing these services. Without your time, there is no service.

Time is not a limiting factor in generating passive income. Selling books or ad space on your own website are examples of passive income. Videos are another great example of a passive product. There may be an upfront time investment in writing a book, developing a website, or shooting a video, but once complete the revenue from that effort can continue whether you are available or not. Passive products allow you to leverage the impact of your efforts. One video can be seen by thousands of people. Social media opens the doors to unlimited promotion of passive income products.

You need to consider different forms of active and passive income appropriate for your own business. You may choose to have only a single income stream such as consulting. You may find over time you can leverage your experience to create other forms of income such as the consultant who writes a book or gets paid for giving speeches. Just be careful your ambitions for other income streams do not get in the way of your primary business.

Know Your Customer Base

Being on your own means you are no longer tied to a corporate policy regarding the *profitability of a customer*. You can chase the small fry as well as the larger better-funded organizations. You decide who your customers are going to be. A financial planner I met felt quite liberated once he left a corporate environment so that he could provide services for people with lesser means rather than constantly chasing the proverbial whale. You can do good things for your clients, but do not forget your bottom line so that you can continue to do good things.

Identifying your potential customer base is an important step. It determines the size of your market, the way you reach your customers, and elements of the sales cycle.

Conduct market research to make sure a large enough market exists that might use a new company's offering. Selling your expertise on pay phone installation might prove a challenging business with the limited number of pay phones these days. Type writer repair? Also a declining market.

The New Enterprise Forum (NEF) created an excellent piece on defining your market size.[2] NEF is dedicated to helping entrepreneurs get ready for talking to investors so the article is written for expressing market size to investors, but it can be applied to help you identify your serviceable market. In full disclosure, I am on the NEF Board of Directors as one of my volunteer/networking activities.

---

[2]   http://newenterpriseforum.org/sites/default/files/resources/NEF_Market_ Size_Estimation.pdf

Many easily accessible sources of information are available over the Internet or at your local library. Some common ones include:

- Federal government statistics websites
  o https://sba.gov/advocacy/firm-size-data
  o https://census.gov/econ/ (updates every year)
  o https://census.gov/programs-surveys/susb.html
- State government statistics websites
  o http://milmi.org/datasearch (for Michigan)
- Industry/trade organizations online
  o https://nam.org/state-manufacturing-data/
    (for manufacturing data)

Library resources—Many of the sites below charge for information but your local library might already pay for a subscription service that you can use for free. This is particularly true of larger business school libraries.

- Gartner Reports
  o http://gartner.com
- Risk Management Association
  o http://rmahq.org/ (look under the Knowledge Center tab)
- Plunkett Research
  o https://plunkettresearch.com/
- Standard & Poor's Net Advantage
  o Available through a library affiliation
- Dun & Bradstreet
  o http://dnb.com/
- Reference USA
  o http://resource.referenceusa.com/
- InfoUSA (lists of potential clients)
  o www.infousa.com

A good starting point point in determining your customer base is to ask the following questions:

1. What size companies do you want to be selling to?
   Anything from individuals up to Fortune 500 behemoths
2. Who in the company do you need to be selling to?
   IT manager, CFO, Marketing Director…

3. What industry do you want to be selling to?
   Manufacturers, Service Providers, Hair Dressers, Hospitals
4. What geographical territory will you cover?
   Your city, your state…

If your answers to these questions is anything like: all sizes, every-one in the organization, all industries, and world-wide, *please* rethink your position. As a solopreneur, you need to focus. You do not have the bandwidth (or probably even the service offerings) to satisfy all of these constituencies.

If your target market is the Fortune 500, they are easy to identify but challenging to reach and will present a longer sales cycle. If your target is dry cleaners on your street, you can easily find them but the market potential may be too small. Online resources will help you identify the quantity of businesses in certain geographic areas. Fortunately, it does not take too many clients to keep a sole practitioner consultant busy. You do not need to sell thousands or millions of widgets. So how large is your potential market (number of possible customers)?

Know Your Customer

LaRue Hosmer, a former University of Michigan Business School professor, once told my class that if our customer was to walk in the door right now, we should be able to describe them in detail. The answer I developed for my consulting practice is:

The owner or CFO of a manufacturing company with 50 to 100 employees still using QuickBooks and/or a paper-based system to man-age their inventory, production control and finances located within driving distance from my home.

That one sentence defines the industry I know, tells me the company is large enough to afford my services, I am addressing the key decision maker, and he or she has a need that I can provide value in satisfying. My geographic target area contains over 10,000 manufacturing businesses matching that size requirement. I need to work with less than 0.1 percent of them each year to be quite successful. That is a manageable target.

Marketing people like to talk about a customer persona. A persona is a fictional representation of a potential customer. You develop a persona based on research to incorporate the needs, goals, and behavior patterns of your target market. Depending on the complexity of your services, you may need to develop multiple personas to represent distinct types of potential clients. A quick search on the Internet provides multiple sites with further information on persona development.

Using my example from above and applying the concepts of developing a persona might result in something like this:

> *George, age 52, is the owner of ABC Stamping Company which was founded by his dad in his garage thirty years ago. The business, located in Jackson, MI, has 62 employees and an old-time bookkeeper who sends out the invoices and pays the bills. The bookkeeper tracks all their financial transactions in Excel and provides the spreadsheets to the accountants each quarter. George is constantly frustrated by the difficulty in finding information or getting reports. He thinks he is making money because he must pay taxes every year but wonders why he is constantly running low on cash. He expects the bookkeeper will retire within the next three years and is concerned about how to capture her knowledge before she leaves.*

I could go on but you hopefully get the point.
How would you describe your customer?
Can you develop your own customer persona(s)?

Many other firms offer the same services that I do. Some of them are large consulting and accounting organizations. I see my competitive advantage as the following:

- My experience—large firms throw newly minted MBAs at a project with minimal software or manufacturing experience.
- My tool set—I use proprietary tools and a process that has been proven over many engagements.
- My target market—many firms are looking for the large Oracle or SAP kinds of projects that pay millions of dollars for consultants. My client projects (and clients) are much smaller and use less complicated software systems.

- My independence—I am unbiased and not tied to any software product so I represent the best interests of my client. Many competitors are tied to specific software applications.
- My flexibility—as a one-person shop, I have the power to make all of the decisions and can respond to each customer's specific needs in a unique way.

Why will someone choose to hire you? Think about the competitive advantage you have in offering your services. Why will someone pick you over all the other marketplace alternatives? Price? Quality of work? Availability? Track record and references? How are you going to communicate that advantage to your potential customers?

You need to determine what makes the value of your services better than your competitors. How would you describe your competitive advantage in selling to your customer?

On the topic of customers, not every customer is a good customer. In fact, there are customers out there that you want to avoid. The best example is the customer who never pays you. During your sales process (more in Chapter 10) you need to qualify the customers to make sure they are people you want as clients. It is your business and you choose to work or not work with anyone you want. Here are a few of the situations you need to avoid.

1. The non-paying customer. Later on, this book addresses how to get customers to pay you, but that assumes they have the money to do so. As part of your qualification process you need to make sure the company is financially secure enough to pay you. That is not a problem if you are doing work for Ford Motor Company but maybe it is if your client is Ford Embroidery (made up fictional name so no slight inferred). Feel free to ask for credit references before starting a project.

2. Personality disorders or behavioral issues. You do not need a client who is always yelling at you, putting you down and telling you your work is not good enough. You do not need a client who harasses you in any manner. These behavior patterns are not always obvious during an initial interaction so try to talk with other employees as well before making a full commitment.

3. No focus or priorities. Unless your task is to help them identify and set priorities, these types of clients are difficult. Every meeting sends you off in a different direction, and project scope creep becomes a genuine issue. Deadlines gets drawn out as other projects become the idea of the day.

4. Ethical issues or other nonalignment of principles. If your client is asking you to do something that you are not comfortable in doing, perhaps you need to walk away. For example, a client might ask you to provide confidential marketing information about a company where you were previously employed. Not only could you potentially be facing legal issues from the prior employer but you would also be compromising your values. Do not cross that line! (See Chapter 13 on ethics.)

5. Dominating ego. A clear warning sign is when a customer thinks his or her needs always go in front of the rest of your clients to the point of the other clients' detriment. You need to balance all your customers' needs and priorities. If you allow one customer to totally dominate you, you will soon have only one customer.

Hopefully, you identify these situations before they occur or can head them off if you have already started an engagement.

Chapter 4: Homework
Update the notebook you are keeping with the following:
- Describe your service offering in 25 words or less. This is your opener when you first meet people and they ask you what you do. Be informative and create a hook so that they want to learn more about your services.
- Do your market research.
  o Determine the size of the target market that you can realistically attack.
- Expand on your customer narrative from Chapter 3 to describe your ideal customer.
  o Develop the customer persona(s).
- Define your competitive advantage in pursuing your target market.

CHAPTER 5

Forming a Legal Business Entity

A Company Limited? What may that be? The term, I rather think, is new to me.
>   —King Paramount, Gilbert & Sullivan's *Utopia Limited*

From all of the new business startups each year, less than 10 percent are formed as corporations. Corporations and limited liability companies (LLCs) are both legal entities, separate and distinct from the people who create and own them. Sole proprietorships are not. Corporations have shareholders. LLCs have members. Sole proprietorships simply refer to a person who owns the business and is responsible for its debts. Many reasons exist why you need to form a legal entity for your business. Chief among those are:

- Structured properly, you cannot be held personally responsible for the debts of the business. This allows you to sign legal documents on behalf of the business without personal exposure, but you need to keep a clear distinction between business and personal assets. Providing a personal guarantee for a business loan, offering your private property as collateral, or simply signing a contract in your own name exposes your personal assets. (Sign contracts as Joe Smith, Member of ABC, LLC.)
- To protect your business name. Someone else can start a similar business with the same name, and you would have no recourse. Potentially, they could force you to stop using that name. Simply registering your name with your city or county only provides protection within that narrow geographic range.

- To establish a true business entity recognized by the state and federal government. This allows you to use your federal Employer Identification Number (EIN) instead of your social security number for business needs. In a world where cyber-security breaches are common, the fewer people having your social security number, the better. Some banks require you to have an EIN in order to set up a business checking account.
- To provide the perception of a bona fide business. Being able to add the LLC or Inc. designation at the end of your company name tells the world you are serious about your company and have taken the necessary steps to get it formally recognized.
- To make you think about the long-term structure of your business.
  o Will you be taking on partners?
  o Do you expect your income to go above six figures?
  o Do you understand the liabilities and responsibilities that come with a genuine business?

There are different corporate structures you can choose from when starting a business. Michigan's Small Business Development Center has an excellent description of the options for companies formed in Michigan[1] and other states have comparable sites.

Talk to a lawyer or accountant who makes sure you get started correctly or use a legal services website such as www.legalshield.com or www.legalzoom.com.

Option 0: Do Zero

The worst option is to do nothing. The risk in doing nothing is that a creditor would have access to both your personal and business assets. You end up with very limited protection of your company's assets, such as your company name, or your personal assets. If you are sued for business reasons, your personal assets are also at risk.

---

[1]   http://sbdcmichigan.org/guidetostarting

Option 1: Sole Proprietorship

At a minimum, you should form a sole proprietorship by registering your business with your city or county as "doing business as" (DBA); such as Joe Smith doing business as Joe's Consulting Emporium. The fee should be negligible, and your business income and expenses are managed on your Federal Income Tax Form 1040 Schedule C. This provides some protection for your company name, but only within the county or city where you have registered. Whether you register as a sole proprietor or not, your net earnings are subject to all self-employment taxes (see Chapter 6) and income taxes.

Option 2: LLC

The next step up the ladder is to create an LLC. As Gilbert & Sullivan fans learned in the operetta *Utopia Limited*, this structure is based entirely on the concept of the corporate shield provided by a limited liability entity. The LLC concept originated in Germany in 1892 and has now spread to much of the world. As recently as 1977, Wyoming became the first state in the United States to enact what we recognize today as a single-person LLC entity. It was quickly followed by other states.

The concept of today's LLC is to protect an individual's personal assets in the event the business is sued. But, this works in the opposite direction as well, protecting your company assets against any personal actions. The cost to form an LLC varies by state (Michigan is currently $50; California is $800 plus fees). Once you have formed an LLC, filing the annual report with your state (including a filing fee) is all that is required to keep it active.

For tax purposes, a single-person LLC (or a husband and wife filing a joint return) is a *disregarded entity*. This means you still use the Form 1040 Schedule C to report your business net income and still need to pay the self-employment taxes. Some states do impose additional taxes and fees on LLC businesses. The tax treatment is different in community property and non-community property states (for husband and wife joint returns). Check with your accountant to see if any of these issues apply in your state.

Adding a second partner to your LLC business makes the federal tax reporting more complicated with the addition of K-1 and 1065 forms required. If you plan to have multiple business owners or investors, an LLC is not your best option. In one situation, an employee invested money in an LLC organization in exchange for 30 percent of the profits. Not much later, the business went bankrupt. The LLC owner had put all of the business assets into his own private account rather than that of the business. The investor had no recourse against the owner, and there were no assets of value left in the LLC. Moral of the story, do not invest money in an LLC unless you are confident about the ownership of the assets.

Once you have formed your LLC, avoid the following situations to maintain a clear separation of business and personal assets:

- Signing a personal guarantee for the business. This means you are obligated to pay personally if your business is unable to.
- Offering your property as collateral. If the bank wants you to put up your house as collateral for the business loan, walk away.
- Signing a contract under your own name. After your name, always include words similar to Owner, ABC LLC. You are only signing on behalf of the LLC.
- Mixing of personal and business accounts. Keep separate checking and credit card accounts for your business and personal lives.
- Fraud, misrepresentation, or sloppy bookkeeping. If you lied in order to get a loan or credit for your business, you can still be held personally responsible.

Creating an LLC organization requires you to identify a registered (or resident) agent. This is the person identified by your company to officially receive and send papers on your behalf, including annual state filings. Usually, the registered agent needs to be a resident within the state(s) where you are registered or a corporation authorized to do business within the state. You can be the registered agent for your own business or you can identify a third party.

If you choose to register your LLC in the state you live and act as the registered agent, you do not have legal LLC protection when doing business in another state. Third-party agents can make sure you are properly registered in any state where you do business, and any online inquiries about your business formation only shows the registered agent's information and not yours. Make sure you find a reputable agent you can trust and not just an online service looking to make a fast buck.

One LLC had a registered agent that left the business (and the state) during a downturn in the economy. Legal documents were sent to the old address, but never found their way to the LLC. The end result was the state dropping the LLC's business registration and the loss of licensing rights. The moral here is to periodically make sure your registered agent is still in business, serving your needs.

While it may not be required in your state, it is a wise idea to create an operating agreement for your LLC. California, Delaware, Missouri, Nebraska, and New York currently required one for single-member LLCs. Sample agreements can be found online but most contain many of the following sections:

1. Organization
   a. Formation and business purpose
   b. Name and address
   c. Resident agent
   d. Term (usually indefinite)
   e. Named member(s) of the business
   f. Disability or death of the named member
2. Capital contribution
   a. Initial contribution
   b. Additional contributions
3. Profit, losses, and distribution
4. Management
   a. Powers of the member, including voting, signing contracts, and so on
   b. Member liability
   c. Indemnification
   d. Records

5. Compensation

6. Bookkeeping

7. Dissolution

For a single-person LLC, this seems like overkill because only one person is involved in the company and all decision making. But, think of an operating agreement like a will for your company. This is a legal document. Without one, if the single member becomes disabled or dies, your state gets to decide the fate of the organization. That could be very costly to the business and surviving dependents. Again, using a lawyer or specialist in this area costs some money up front, but can save you considerably more money down the road.

If you plan to do business in more than one state, you are advised to file foreign LLC paperwork in those other states. The term *foreign* just means the LLC was originally formed outside the state in which you intend to do business. The first state where you register your business is the *domestic LLC*; all succeeding states are registered as *foreign LLCs*. Without it, a lawyer or creditor in those states can pierce the veil of your LLC protection. The states themselves may also impose fines and penalties. The cost is usually the same as creating an LLC in those states.

If I was going to another state to conduct a four-hour training session, I would not worry about filling a foreign LLC. If I landed a $100k consulting job in California, I would definitely file the foreign LLC paperwork, or the state might impose a hefty penalty. Educate yourself on the risks you face when you conduct business in other states. Just one more reason to have a good corporate attorney you can turn to for information.

Option 3: Corporation

Finally, you can form a corporation. This provides a whole other layer of protection between your personal and business assets, but comes with additional costs as well. A corporation is a separate legal entity that transacts business under its own name, files separate corporate income tax forms, has shareholders (at least one), and, quite frequently, employees.

The corporate structure has a number of requirements, including the need for by-laws, annual meetings, and recording of minutes.

One relatively new corporate structure is a B Corp, which is also known as a low-profit LLC (L3C) in some states. This is limited to companies that have an educational or charitable purpose. Consulting may be educational, but talk to your lawyer before going ahead and registering under this banner.

S-Corporation shareholders are taxed on their share of corporate profits. Before profits can be distributed, a *reasonable salary* must be paid to any owner-employee. This can save some money because the distribution of profits is not subject to the self-employment tax, but there are additional legal and accounting fees for managing this structure. This structure makes more sense for businesses with multiple owners and larger incomes (certainly over $100,000).

C-Corporations are taxable entities. This means the corporation must pay taxes on any net income in addition to the individual income taxes. When I started my own consulting practice, I incorporated as a C-Corporation. This was done so that I was able to deduct my *employee benefit expenses* as a business expense. Those expenses included my medical, dental, and vision insurance costs, which were high enough to offset the added year-end tax forms and other reporting expenses. The changes in health care reform eliminated this issue, and I dissolved the corporation. Now I am an LLC.

While there is nothing wrong with being a sole proprietor, if your business is sued for any reason, the plaintiff can come after your personal assets, not just business assets. Talk to your accountant and your lawyer, but see if you are not best served by being a single-person LLC business.

Once you have formed a legal entity, you should apply for a federal EIN. The EIN is also known as a Federal Tax Identification Number and is used to identify a business entity. Many entities (customers on W-9 forms, banks in setting up checking accounts, etc.) require either your social security number or EIN. If you hire employees or use subcontractors (in excess of $600), you need an EIN. Using an EIN helps to protect your social security number and adds a level of professionalism to your business. Best of all, getting an EIN is a free service of the IRS. To get your EIN, start at https://irs.gov/Businesses/Small-Businesses-&-Self-Employed/ Employer-ID-Numbers-EINs

Chapter 5: Homework
Update your notebook with the following as appropriate:
- Talk to your attorney! I cannot emphasize this enough.
  o Set up your legal business structure.
  o Create an operating plan.
  o Get your EIN.
- Find and talk to an expert experienced in structuring business startups.
  o Attorneys are good with legal documents, but there are other issues to consider as well.

PART II

What You Need to Understand About Your Financials

CHAPTER 6

Income, Expenses, and the Tax Man

Money is better than poverty, if only for financial reasons.

—Woody Allen

Understanding and Forecasting Your Expenses

It is important your business income (along with any other money coming in) is sufficient to cover your living expenses, so a short discussion on income and expenses is in order.

Consultants may dream of high six-figure incomes, but the reality is much harsher for most. It is important to know how much money you need to maintain your current standard of living or whether you need to be cutting back in certain areas. The Consumer Expenditures Report, updated annually in September by the U.S. Department of Labor Bureau of Labor Statistics, shows the following income and spending breakdown for an *average* U.S. household (Table 6.1).

The average household had 2.5 people, 1.9 cars, and 1.3 wage earners. The average age of the person completing the survey was 50.1 years old.

If you, like the residents of Garrison Keillor's Lake Wobegon, consider yourself above average (or at least inspire to be so), then your income and many of the expenses are even higher. Modify these numbers based on your personal situation and do not forget to add in any monthly debt payments for car or college loans. (It is easy to understand why the average person has trouble saving money for their kids' college tuition.) Unless your spouse has coverage, you may need to pay for medical and dental insurance.

Table 6.1 Average household income and expenses[1]

	2015	2016	2017	2018
Average Income before taxes	$69,627	$74,664	$73,573	$78,635
Average Spending				
Housing	$18,409	$18,886	$19,884	$20,091
Food	$7,023	$7,203	$7,729	$7,923
Apparel and services	$1,846	$1,803	$1,833	$1,866
Transportation	$9,503	$9,049	$9,576	$9,761
Healthcare	$4,342	$4,612	$4,928	$4,968
Entertainment	$2,842	$2,913	$3,203	$3,226
Personal Care	$683	$707	$762	$768
Education	$1,315	$1,329	$1,491	$1,407
Cash Donations	$1,819	$2,081	$1,873	$1,888
Personal Insurance/ pensions	$6,349	$6,831	$6,771	$7,296
All Other	$1,847	$1,897	$2,010	$2,030
Total Expenses	$55,978	$57,311	$60,060	$61,224

On top of these, there are new expenses for operating your company. Some examples include the following one time or annual costs.

Networking events	$300–500; which does not include large trade shows
Marketing material	$250; higher at startup—business cards, brochures
New website	$1,500–5,000; this can be a big upfront expense
Sales travel	$500–2,000; depends how far you are willing to travel
Professional fees	$500–2,000; accounting services for sure, lawyer probably
Liability insurance	$200–1,000; depending on your service offering

---

[1] https://bls.gov Economic Releases→Latest Releases→Archived News Releases→ Consumer Expenditures Surveys

Managing Your Finances

You need to set up a separate checking account and credit card for your business. It is important to keep your business transactions separate from your personal money.

I set up a checking account under the name of my business. The money I get from customers goes directly into the business bank account (usually the checks are made out to my business name). Whenever I need money, I simply transfer funds from my *business* account to my *personal* account. I also have a credit card just for business expenses. Each month, I pay off the balance on the card from my business checking account. This makes it very clean to identify my business expenses at year end.

You want to minimize using cash for business transactions whenever possible so that you can maintain a solid audit trail. Keep track of minor cash transactions (parking meters) that do not have any backup paperwork—these can add up! Collect receipts whenever possible. Without documentation, it is much harder to prove you had an actual business expense. Save receipts, invoices, bank and credit card statements, and any other written proof of what you have spent.

In addition to your checkbook and credit card statements, track your income and expense in an Excel spreadsheet (see Table 6.2) or a similar tool. The various categories to track will be discussed in more detail later in this chapter. If your business has only three to six invoices per month, this type of tool is simple to use. If your business model has a large number of transactions, consider using a software program such as QuickBooks, Xero (for Mac users), Wave, or one of the many other low-end accounting packages. There are a variety of mobile apps that are useful in keeping track of mileage and other business expenses such as Everlance, MileIQ, and so on. Fortunately, the cost of these programs can be deducted as a business expense.

Table 6.2 Sample business budget template

	January	February	March	April	May	June	July	August	September	October	November	December	Total
Income													
Client A	1000	1000	1000	1000	1000	1000	1000	1000	1000	1000	1000	1000	12,000
Client B	5000			5000			5000			5000			20,000
Client C	1000	1000	1000	1000	1000								5,000
Client D	500	500	500	500	500	500	500	500	500	500	500	500	6,000
New Clients			1000	2000	3000	4000	5000	5000	7000	8000	9000	10000	54,000
Total	$7,500	$2,500	$3,500	$9,500	$5,500	$5,500	$11,500	$6,500	$8,500	$14,500	$10,500	$11,500	$97,000

	January	February	March	April	May	June	July	August	September	October	November	December	Total
Expenses													
Advertising			5000						500				5,500
Vehicle Expense	1500	1500	1500	1500	1500	1500	1500	1500	1500	1500	1500	1500	18,000
Subcontractors													0
Insurance								500					500
Legal Fees	500				500				500				1,500
Accounting Fees				5000									5,000
Office Supplies	100	100	100	100	100	100	100	100	100	100	100	100	1,200
Home Office Expense													0
Repairs			250			250			250			250	1,000
Supplies	50	50	50	50	50	50	50	50	50	50	50	50	600
Taxes & Licenses			250										250
Travel	1000		2000	1000			1000			1000			6,000
Meals	500	500	500	500	500	500	500	500	500	500	500	500	6,000
Telephone	200	200	200	200	200	200	200	200	200	200	200	200	2,400
Internet	150	150	150	150	150	150	150	150	150	150	150	150	1,800
Total	$4,000	$2,500	$10,000	$8,500	$3,000	$2,750	$3,500	$3,000	$3,750	$3,500	$2,500	$2,750	$49,750
Net income	$3,500	$0	-$6,500	$1,000	$2,500	$2,750	$8,000	$3,500	$4,750	$11,000	$8,000	$8,750	$47,250

Notice, in Table 6.2, that while the year, as a whole, is quite positive, there is a negative cashflow in March and an outflow of money through April. It is important you understand the financial impact your life choice decision will have on your finances.

Creating a Budget

As mentioned earlier, running out of cash is a top reason why businesses fail. Creating a budget will help to identify where cash will be tight and how you are doing against your plan.

One way to attack this is to use a similar spreadsheet to create an annual budget for your family's spending (see Table 6.3). You and your significant other need to agree on the results of the budgeting process. This provides an excellent communication tool to track your expectations against reality.

Develop your budget by looking first at what you spent last year. Many of these expenses reoccur monthly such as mortgage or rent payments, utility bills, and groceries. Add an expense line for each category you wish to track. See if you need to eliminate any one-time expenses or add any new ones. Do you really need a trip to Disney World every year? Make sure you capture the large one- or two-time payments such as property taxes or insurance. Try to track all your expenses and categorize them in a manner that is useful for you. That covers the expense side.

Forecasting your revenue is harder. You may have income from other sources such as a spouse's salary, but unless you already have clients lined up, business income may not start or come in as quickly as you expect. Starting a new business is not easy. Assume customers do not pay you for at least 30 days from when you send the invoice. Try to be conservative in your income projections. If money comes in sooner than expected, surely, you can deal with that problem!

Now comes the important part—comparing your income to your expense projections. If your income looks like it covers all your expenses, that is great! When income is not sufficient to cover expenses, you have a problem and usually start to eat into your savings. One option is to go over your expenses again to see what can be cut out or reduced. Another option, although harder, is to figure out how to increase the income number. At a minimum, you want to end up with a balanced budget where the income equals the expenses. It is not critical every month be balanced, but you certainly want to avoid running in the hole for extended periods of time.

The example in Table 6.3 shows almost $8,000 available at year end, but there was a drawdown of more than $15,000 during the year. If this cannot be reconciled, the money will need to come from your savings or be borrowed. Make sure your family is onboard with this plan.

The last step with any budget is to monitor and update it. Look at it each month, add actual values for the month that just passed, and make any necessary changes to future projections. If the revenue numbers are falling significantly short of your expectations, you will be glad you already developed a financial contingency plan.

Once again, the trick is to make sure your income is greater than your expenses or determine how you can fund the gap if one exists. Running out of cash is the quickest way to business ruin and family squabbles.

One other very useful tool is a business calendar. This can be a hard copy or electronic version such as Outlook or Google Calendar. Beyond the normal function of reminding you of upcoming appointments in the coming days or weeks, a calendar also acts as a diary to record where you were and with whom you met. This is very useful in providing documentation to justify certain business expenses. For example, if your calendar shows a client lunch meeting downtown last month, then it is reasonable you expensed the cost of the meal and round-trip business mileage from your house or office to that meeting.

Understanding Your Income

Most solopreneur consultants operate on a cash basis, which means you (and the IRS) recognize the revenue or income from your business once you receive payment from your customer, not when you do the work or invoice the customer. The difference in timing may not seem significant until you have clients who drag their feet and do not pay right away.

With a full-time job, you do the work and the paychecks come on a regular basis. As a consultant, you do the work and may not see the

Table 6.3 Sample family budget template

Income	January	February	March	April	May	June	July	August	September	October	November	December	Total
Business Income	7500	2500	3500	9500	5500	5500	11500	6500	8500	14500	10500	11500	97,000
Your Income													
Spouse's Income													
Interest	50	50	50	50	50	50	50	50	50	50	50	50	600
Other Income	1000	1000	1000	1000	1000	6000	1000	1000	1000	1000	1000	1000	17,000
Total	$8,550	$3,550	$4,550	$10,550	$6,550	$11,550	$12,550	$7,550	$9,550	$15,550	$11,550	$12,550	$ 1,14,600

Expenses	January	February	March	April	May	June	July	August	September	October	November	December	Total
Business Expenses	4000	2500	10000	8500	3000	2750	3500	3000	3750	3500	2500	2750	49,750
Mortgage	1600	1600	1600	1600	1600	1600	1600	1600	1600	1600	1600	1600	19,200
Groceries	650	650	650	650	650	650	650	650	650	650	650	650	7,800
Auto Expense	800	800	800	800	800	800	800	800	800	800	800	800	9,600
Clothing	120	120	120	120	120	120	120	120	120	120	120	120	1,440
Insurance										2500			2,500
Electric Bills	200	200	200	200	200	200	200	200	200	200	200	200	2,400
Telephone Bills	50	50	50	50	50	50	50	50	50	50	50	50	600
Cable Bills	266	266	266	266	266	266	266	266	266	266	266	266	3,192
Medical Bills	410	410	410	410	410	410	410	410	410	410	410	410	4,920
Vacations									2500				2,500
Kid's Schooling	125	125	125	125	125	125	125	125	125	125	125	125	1,500
Credit Card other													0
Other Expenses	100	100	100	100	100	100	100	100	100	100	100	100	1,200
TOTAL	$8,321	$6,821	$14,321	$12,821	$7,321	$7,071	$7,821	$7,321	$10,571	$10,321	$6,821	$7,071	$1,06,602
NET INCOME	$229	-$3,271	-$9,771	-$2,271	-$771	$4,479	$4,729	$229	-$1,021	$5,229	$4,729	$5,479	$7,998

payment for several months. Meanwhile, many of your personal monthly expenses continue. This can create a cash crunch, so be prepared particularly when first getting started.

Another acceptable accounting method is the accrual method. This means you recognize expenses and income based on billings, not cash receipts. As soon as you bill your customer (or receive a vendor's invoice), you recognize the revenue (or expense). While the accrual method does not change the actual timing of your cashflow, it enables you to accelerate your expenses (vendor invoice receipt date rather than payment date).

For most solopreneur consultants, the accrual method only accelerates your taxable income without accelerating enough additional expenses. Consult with your accountant for guidance on your accounting methodology.

After the end of the year, plan on receiving 1099-MISC forms from many of your customers. They are required to do so by the IRS for payments made to non-corporate entities exceeding $600. If your client has you complete a W-9, you should expect a 1099-MISC form. A W-9 is like a W-4, providing your customer (rather than your employer) with your federal tax ID information.

Make sure you save all the 1099-MISC forms you receive. Your Schedule C income should equal or exceed the total amount of the 1099-MISC forms (customers do not need to send them to you if you did less than $600 of work). A few exceptions may occur where amounts reported by your customer were not received by you until the following year (they pay on December 30, but you do not receive the check until January 2), and therefore, not part of your prior year's taxable income. This is a shortcoming of a cash-basis business, but you should be able to reconcile the differences. You may even be able to use this to your tax advantage to delay reportable income by requesting your customers hold off on late year payments until the following year.

The IRS will check the total of the 1099-MISC forms against your reported income.

Understanding Your Taxes, the Bad News

While this book is not intended to provide tax advice, and a good accountant is a critical resource for any business owner, there are a few general tips and tricks to share.

The IRS targets sole proprietors for audits every year, with the belief that this group routinely under-reports revenue and over-reports business expenses. While the total number of audits is a small percentage to the total tax returns filled, if audited, your best defense is a well-documented record of all of your revenue and expenses.

Full-time employees have their federal, state, social security, and Medicare taxes automatically deducted from the paycheck. In addition, the company pays other taxes, such as the unemployment tax. Individuals on their own need to pay some of these company taxes.

Unless you have decided to form a corporation (see Chapter 5), as your own boss, you do not need to give yourself a paycheck. Nonetheless, you do need to be concerned about paying tax on the money or income you receive during the course of the year. You must make quarterly tax deposits to both the federal government and your local state government if applicable (some states have no income tax). The payments to the Feds include money for your income taxes as well as money for social security and Medicare (FICA). When working as an employee, you had money deducted from your paycheck to cover your share of FICA. Your employer also paid its share. The kick in the butt is now you have to pay both halves of FICA or a total of 15.3 percent of your net income (at higher income levels, that percentage changes). You may get some of this back when you file your taxes, but that does not help the cashflow during the year.

To avoid penalties, you must pay quarterly installments totaling at least as much as you owed in taxes the previous year or enough to cover 90 percent of your tax bill for the current year. If your income is significantly less than what you made working full-time the previous year, there is no reason to fork over the same amount for taxes during the current year. Your accountant is your best guide on your quarterly payments.

Understanding Your Taxes, the Good News

The recently passed Tax Cuts and Job Act provided a new tax deduction for passthrough entities such as sole proprietorships. The deduction generally provides a 20 percent deduction on your personal tax return for qualified business income. Limitations apply based on the type of business and your total income, but getting a potential 20 percent income deduction is a nice present from the government.

As you are now running your own business, a number of your current expenses may fall under a business expense category. You still need to put up the cash to pay your bills, but these expenses are a deduction from your business income at tax time. It is, therefore, very important to keep track of your various business expenses during the year. This is on you. The IRS will not audit you because you did not take enough business expense deductions.

It is equally important to know what expenses are not allowed as deductions by the IRS. As a general rule of thumb, the IRS allows any business expenses that are ordinary and necessary in the operation of your business (sorry, that new business suit you bought to impress clients does not qualify as a uniform). The IRS does not let you deduct certain expenses, but you should avoid these whenever possible (bribes, fines for violation of the law—even parking tickets, and so on).

For every $1,000 in legitimate business expense, you can save yourself from $120 to $400 depending on your federal and state tax rates. This savings is there only to the extent that your business is profitable. If you have $10,000 of business income and $15,000 of business expense, the last $5,000 in expenses does not save you on taxes (at least in the current year). If your business is constantly losing money, talk to your tax advisor to make sure the IRS qualifies what you are doing as a business, and not just a hobby.

Set up an Excel spreadsheet to track your business expenses, as they need to be reported to the IRS. These can be found by downloading the IRS Schedule C form, Profit and Loss from Business. While you can track expenses in whatever way is meaningful to you, eventually, you need to summarize them on the Schedule C. For example, it may benefit your business to track your legal expenses and accounting expenses separately, but Schedule C only has one line for professional services.

The Schedule C instructions provide some guidance on the various areas of expense and some of them are further elaborated below.

Inventory: The purchase cost of inventory is a business expense in the period when you sell that inventory. Most consultants do not have inventory, but perhaps, you are a self-published author with a bestseller on your hands. The books could be treated as inventory and expensed in the year they are sold.

Advertising: Do you pay for a premium LinkedIn account? Do you attend networking events with a fee? Did you pay for website development and hosting? This is all advertising or marketing.

Car and truck expense: Unless you have a vehicle dedicated solely to your business, a luxury few can afford, you need to keep track of your actual mileage driven for any business purpose, including sales calls, onsite work, networking events, going to the bank to deposit your checks, and so on. Every year, the IRS comes up with a standard mileage rate you can use to calculate the deductible costs for using your vehicle for business. The 2020 rate is $0.575 per mile (the 2019 rate was $0.58 per mile). So, for every 1,000 miles you drove for business in 2019, you have $580 of deductible expense. The current rate can be found on the IRS website and is based on an annual study of automobile operating costs, which change as gasoline and other prices fluctuate.

Contract labor: Rather than hire employees, you can subcontract work and avoid certain headaches. You need to make sure you comply with IRS rules regarding employees versus contractors. Most of these relate to who controls how and where the work gets done.

Insurance: Here is where you can expense any liability insurance you purchased for your business activities.

Legal and professional fees: If you were already paying an accountant, now you have a legitimate reason to book the fees as a business expense. If you used a lawyer to set up your business or review business contracts, those fees are also deductible.

Office supplies: This can range from printer paper to a paper shredder; all the normal business supplies you would need, as well as the postage your business uses. This covers all the office supplies your family should ever need.

Home office expense: This is a tricky one. I do not expense much for my home office, as it is small and I use it for other purposes than just business. Large home office expenses can attract the attention of the IRS (so I have been told), but if it is legit, go for it!

Repairs and maintenance: When your business computer breaks down and you need to have the hard drive replaced, this expense is covered.

Supplies: You can deduct the cost of books, professional instruments, equipment, and so on if you normally use them within the year.

Taxes and licenses: This covers my annual report filing expense with the State of Michigan. You may have additional items.

Travel: This includes lodging and transportation connected with overnight travel for business, but can cover some of your normal travel costs as well. I have family in the Minneapolis area. I fly into Minneapolis on a Thursday, conduct business meetings on Friday, and return home on Sunday. The cost of my airline ticket is fully deductible, as well as at least one night of hotel accommodation. Renting a car would be partially deductible.

Meals and entertainment: The IRS has some pretty strict rules on what are allowed expenses in this category and only allows for a 50 percent deduction of those expenses.

Utilities: Do you have a second phone line that you use for your business? It could even be your cell phone so that cost can be expensed.

Wages: If you hire employees, you can deduct their wages, but there are numerous other forms to complete and fees to pay (unemployment tax being one example). Part of having a lifestyle business is avoiding the headaches of employees.

You can achieve certain tax advantages by paying your children for legitimate work they do for your business. They are probably in a lower tax bracket than you and, if under 18 years old, with a few exceptions, you do not have to worry about them having to pay FICA or unemployment taxes. Maybe they design your website, run your social media campaign, or even just answer phones and schedule appointments during their summer vacations.

One other tax note regarding Form 1099-MISC. If you paid anyone during the year more than $600 for their services, you are required to complete a 1099-MISC for that individual. Collect their tax information by having them complete a W-9 Form *before they start* doing the work. Tracking down the information later can be extremely difficult particularly if the person has moved (as many students do).

Record Retention

The IRS states you need to keep tax return records as long as they are needed to prove the income or deductions on your return. In general, that is a three-year period, but it is wise to hold onto your records for six or seven years, such as invoices, bank statements, and so on. The IRS can come after you for up to six years for an audit, and there is no time limitation if they suspect fraudulent activity.

All employment tax records need to be kept for four years, and personnel records kept for at least seven years after the employee has left your company. Records dealing with large asset purchases need to be kept for the life of the asset plus an additional six years.

Never throw away your business tax returns. The same can be said for contracts and loan agreements. You may need these for other reasons than dealing with the IRS such as issues with social security or a potential future lawsuit.

Keep your customer working papers for as long as you believe there is potential additional work with the client. This paperwork far exceeds what you keep for financial or tax reasons. If you have not worked with them for several years, chances are most of your paperwork is obsolete. It is important you keep these records in a secure location (your home office may suffice) and dispose of them properly so that they do not fall into the wrong hands.

All the IRS forms and form instructions mentioned can be found at www.irs.gov/forms-instructions. You should also find out if your state has specific forms you should know about for your business. One other useful site is www.nolo.com, with excellent information on both tax and legal aspects of a small business.

The information in this book is designed to give you an idea of what is possible, not provide tax advice. The rules are subject to change. It is important you have a good tax advisor to guide on this subject. You should start talking to them early in the year to position yourself to maximize the various deductions available to you come tax filing season.

Chapter 6: Homework

Update your notebook with the following:

- Develop a budget
  - o Determine your monthly living expenses
  - o Determine your monthly business expenses
  - o Forecast your business income
- Find a system to track your business income and expenses.
- Set up a business checking account and credit card.
- Find a good accountant you can trust who works with other similar businesses.

CHAPTER 7

Setting Your Prices and Getting Paid

Too many people overvalue what they are not and undervalue what they are.

—Malcolm Forbes

There are several different ways of arriving at what you charge for your services. Common ones include charging by the hour, by the project, or by accomplishing certain milestones. Some people go as far as taking equity in a client company, but that is not recommended for consulting newcomers. Equity will not pay your bills this month (or the next, or the next, or the next…).

Mentioned earlier was the need to be providing a service that your customer values. Your challenge is to translate that value into dollars. The more information you can collect about the value to the client, the better prepared you are to defend your rates. For example, if the work you do allows the company to repurpose an individual (I do not like my work to result in layoffs) who is making $50,000 a year, that is a bottom-line savings to the company. You cannot expect to bill them for the entire savings, but most companies would be willing to spend 10–25 percent of that amount. Do your homework. Identify hard cost savings whenever possible. Soft savings are difficult to quantify, but still provide value. Present your client with a full list of these as well.

Establishing Hourly Rates

You can come up with an hourly rate by going through a series of simple steps. Based on the expense calculations you made in the previous chapter, you should have a decent idea of your target annual income. Divide it by your working hours and multiply that by a work factor. Table 7.1 provides some examples.

Table 7.1 Establishing an hourly rate

Target income		Working hours		Work factor	Hourly rate (rounded)
$75,000	/	2,080	*	3	= $110/hour
$38,000	/	1,040	*	3	= $110/hour
$104,000	/	2,080	*	3	= $150/hour
$208,000	/	3,120	*	3	= $200/hour

In the table, 2080 reflects the straight time billable number of working hours in a year (40 hours per week times 52 weeks). If you plan on working only 20 hours a week, then your working hours will be 1040; 60-hour work weeks translate to 3,120 annual working hours. If you plan on working less than 52 weeks, you need to adjust the number accordingly.

The work factor reflects the reality that you are not able to bill for every hour of the day. You will have downtime for sales and marketing activities, proposal writing, holidays and vacations with your family, and so on. Multiplying you working hours by three assumes only one-third of the actual work hours in the year are billable. If you end up billing more than one-third of your time, your income will exceed your target, which is a positive outcome if you do not mind working the extra hours. Once you have a solid base of business, you can consider dropping the work factor multiplier from 3 to 2. Remember, I am talking about a lifestyle where you do not want to be working 80 hours a week, and even the most diligent and successful individuals need to spend some time on non-billable administrative work and business development.

The next step is a sanity check to make sure you are competitive in the marketplace. Very few consultants are able to charge $500/hour. You do not need to be the lowest price consultant on the market, but you do not want to stray too far outside acceptable norms. Do some benchmarking to see what others are charging. The more generic your service offering, the easier it is to do this. It is fairly easy to get hourly rates for graphical design or web design work, but more difficult to get the rate for someone in a very specialized field.

It is a good idea to review your hourly rate from time to time to see if it needs to be adjusted. In a slower economy, you may need to lower your fees to attract business, while the reverse is true once the economy picks up again.

The question of discounting your hourly rate is a persistent one. If you feel you are properly positioned in the marketplace and are not extra hungry for the work, do not discount. Once you start, you will find most of your work going down the discounted path, thus reducing your income. If presented with a project that takes a large number of hours each week over a long period, you may be tempted to discount, but unless you can find more business, you might be locking yourself into a lower income for that period.

Some exceptions do exist. For example, if you really want to do work with a particular client and there is no way they accept your standard rate, discounting may be the only way in the door. Keep the project size small, get the experience you want, and move on.

One of the advantages of charging by the hour is the protection you get if the job grows beyond the initial project scope. If the work load increases, the billable hours increase. Good communications with your customers ensure they understand that project costs are going higher. Many of the hourly rate issues also apply to retainer arrangements.

On the flipside, an hourly rate limits your upside because it is directly tied into the hours you work.

Project Rates

Charging by the project can be cleaner for you and your customer. The timing of payments is specified in advance. Always collect some money early in the project as a sign of good faith from your client and as an indication they are happy with the early progress of the project. This can be an early warning sign if the customer is slow or reluctant to pay.

In coming up with a project fee, you should estimate how many hours the project will take and multiply that by your hourly rate. The result can be modified up or down based on the value of what you are doing, the competitive landscape, your hunger level, and so on.

Charging by the project can provide you with more money IF (and this is a *big if*) you can do the work in less hours than you had estimated for the project. The danger is that it takes you more hours than expected. And, it can end up being a lot more hours. Your timetable for doing work may not be the same as the clients', dragging out the overall project time. You have to be very careful on these projects, accurately communicating with the customer for any work requests going outside the initial project boundaries. This all gets back to good client management.

Larger projects can be broken down into distinct phases, and you can bill each phase as appropriate. My software selection consulting projects have three phases. The first two are fact finding and research. The third is the actual software demos. I charge a flat fee for phases one and two and a daily rate for phase three because the actual number of demos is not known until later in the project.

It is strongly recommended you use a proposal or scope document when billing by the project. This makes the work to be done by the consultant perfectly clear to the customer.

Incentive Clauses

These are not recommended for a start-up consultant. The premise is if certain milestones are met within a given timeframe or other achievements accomplished (e.g., xx percent increase in Web traffic), the customer pays you a bonus. One of the reasons I do not like these is it opens the possibility the customer may request a penalty clause if your work *does not* meet certain guidelines. You do not want to get involved in those types of contracts. When working with a client, there are many issues and potential delays outside your sphere of influence that impact the timing and results of your actual deliverables.

Once you have been in business for a while, you can get more creative and try to build in a bonus element. This may be useful if you get more work than you can manage and are looking to boost your margins on the work you accept. This may work for certain consulting practices, but many industries are not used to doing business that way.

Sweat Equity

If you choose to do work for small start-up companies, many of them do not have much, if any, money to pay you. You may feel good helping these types of businesses, but recognize you are doing a public service. Your chance of the equity ever paying off is very slim.

Those companies do need your help, and they can be a good place to gain both consulting experience and references. On the other hand, they can suck up an enormous amount of your time. Do not plan on a big payday in the future. That is highly unlikely, and they can have an ugly ending. An associate of mine recently got involved with an electric vehicle start-up company only to see a third-party weasel their way in and force the associate out. This was after he had already invested considerable time, energy, and goodwill moving this company forward.

Retainers

While retainers are not really a form of compensation, they are worth mentioning because they are one of the best options for setting the value of your services. It can also be one of the most difficult to initiate. The premise is that, for a fixed billing amount each month, you perform certain tasks for your client. The beauty of this is you know how much time you need to devote to the client each month, you know the amount of money coming from the client each month, and you quickly learn the payment timing schedule of your client.

A retainer make sense when the services you provide are ongoing and not a one-off project. How many websites does your client really need you to build? Bookkeeping, on the other hand, occurs each month. It is much easier to build a business based on services you deliver to your clients on a regular basis. See if you can package your services into repeatable offerings.

One consultant explained to me how he set his retainer rates. He simply figured out how much money he wanted to make for the year and how many clients he wanted to have. The desired annual income divided by number of clients divided by 12 gave him a monthly retainer rate. Fortunately, that number fell in line with what the clients were willing to pay. Make sure you are asking for the market going rate and not getting locked into a long-term low-ball proposal.

Free Work

Once connected in your network, many opportunities will come your way to do work for free. This can lead to paying jobs, but you do not want the reputation as the consultant that works for free. Selling your services is not about giving away your time for free. It is about the exchange of value. Consider working for free only if it is a door opener to paying work with a client, an opportunity to meet key people, or a way to build referrals for your business. Make sure you are not being used and you get the value you are looking for out of the relationship. Once someone is used to getting your services for free, it will be very difficult to later covert them into a paying customer.

In my business, I offer a free half-day assessment. This gets me in the door, I see the problems the company is facing, and I become better positioned to sell my services to the company. This also provides me with data to better define the actual savings I can achieve. I do not offer the same client a second free assessment, as that would have diminishing returns for me. Once they are sold on the value I can provide, they need to pay for that value.

Remember when you are working, you do not have time to be selling, and working for free does not pay the bills.

One final word on setting your price. When you first start your business, you may not have a really good idea on how long a project takes. Maybe you previously did this work in a corporate environment. Maybe it is a skill you learned in school. If you have never done the work as a consultant, you need to learn the reasonable amount of time to complete a *standard* assignment.

Charge a project rate and you will not be paid for any additional hours you need to complete the job—you are unhappy. Charge an hourly rate and the customer may end up paying more than expected—the customer is unhappy. Until you can accurately estimate how long projects take, it is recommended you use an hourly rate. That way, you do not get stuck working for free. If the customer's happiness is very important to you (you may want a good recommendation), you can always make allowances when you bill. That decision is yours, and you get to decide how much of a discount you can afford. One other tip to limit your client's exposure is to state the maximum number of hours you may bill in any one-month time period. That does not necessarily limit the total hours for the project, but does help your customer understand the potential cash outflow.

If you determine more hours (dollars) are needed than the customer expected, talk to your customer. You can explain if extra work got added to the project (scope creep) or if you made an honest mistake in underestimating the amount of the time to complete the project. You may not get paid for all your hours, but might get some compensation without upsetting your customer. Try to find a way where you can get some compensation for the work and still have a happy customer. This is harder to do if you charged a project rate.

Getting Paid

One of the joys of being a sole practitioner is landing new business, but nothing goes down as hard as doing the work and not getting paid (thanks for nothing Mr. K—you know who you are). Additionally, chasing past due accounts is not billable time. Part of the solution is choosing the right customers and part is good upfront communications.

Small start-up companies are usually very low on cash and may be slow to pay. Large companies may have policies about not paying invoices for 60 or more days. You need to make sure you are comfortable with the payment terms before you start any work.

A good proposal document should clearly define the timing and terms for payment. If payments are results-driven, those results must be clearly defined before the engagement begins. Do not wait until the end of a large project to do your billings. Billing once a month is fairly common. You can bill more often if you are incurring large out-of-pocket expenses related to the project (travel, hotels, etc.). Learn your customers' payment pattern. If all invoices are processed and paid on the 25th each month, you do not want to submit your invoice on the 26th.

Credit checking is difficult, but you can request a list of credit references from your client. You need to monitor the outstanding balance owed to you. Are you willing to continue doing work for a client past due in their payments? Two months past due? Three? Four? If you are fortunate enough to have multiple clients, it is easy to overlook a slow payer. A call to your client's project champion is usually sufficient to get the payment ball moving.

Being able to choose your customers is one of the advantages of being the owner of your own business. If they are not paying you in a timely manner, you do not have to work with them.

People take a variety of different approaches, including upfront payments, monthly billings, and credit card processing. For a small fee, you can process a credit card right from your cell phone (via Square or similar service). The easier you make it for the company to pay you, the more likely you are to get paid. Find out each customer's preferences.

A final point. As you are starting and growing your business, you will have many upfront costs required to conduct business. These could include special software applications and computer equipment or even just the cost of your marketing materials. You may have project-specific costs (e.g., travel). These eat into your cashflow, resulting in more money flowing out than flowing in.

To level out your cash flow, it is a prudent idea to get some money upfront at the beginning of any engagement. I know of several people, including a graphical designer, who insist upon full payment before starting any work. (House painters ask for money upfront or get their customers to buy the paint. Very difficult to un-paint a house!) This keeps the cash flow moving in the right direction, helps establish the customer is serious about the project, and eliminates subjective opinions regarding payment for performance (e.g., you create a logo per the client's specifications, but they do not like the design). If you cannot get a token upfront payment from a customer, what is going to happen later when you need to collect on your bill?

Chapter 7: Homework

Update your notebook with the following:

- Determine how much to charge for your services.
  - Compare this to the budgets you developed in Chapter 6.
- Figure out how you will determine the credit worthiness of potential clients.
- Determine how you will invoice for your services.
- Determine your process for chasing after slow paying clients.

PART III

How to Get Customers

CHAPTER 8

Marketing Your Services

You are the product. You feeling something. That's what sells. Not them. Not sex. They can't do what we do, and they hate us for it.
—Don Draper, *Mad Men*

It would be great if your potential customers lined up outside your door like Dairy Queen patrons on a sweltering summer day, but that is usually not the case. You need to generate interest in your business, and marketing is a means to accomplish this. Marketing is not a one-time effort. It needs to be ongoing. Marketing is all about letting people know what you do and not letting them forget about you. How will they still remember you if you take off work for the summer to coach your son's Little League travel baseball team or go on that dream vacation? From content development to networking, marketing tasks are difficult for many of us but, at some level, they need to be done. That requires discipline.

Over the years, I tried to get in the practice of running on a treadmill. It was not until I started tracking my exercise routine on a calendar that I became motivated enough to stick to a program. Looking at my calendar reminded me of the times I had not exercised and motivated me to do better.

The point is to plan and execute a program of activities that is ongoing, persistent, and productive. These marketing tasks can be repeated daily, weekly, monthly, annually, or on an ad-hoc basis. The point is to create a system that tracks the activities you need to be doing and shows your progress. In other words, an activity log. Examples of activity logs are shown in Tables 8.1 and 8.2. Additional activities are highlighted over the next several chapters. One of the biggest challenges you face is not the lack of marketing opportunities, but the ability to choose wisely how to spend your limited time and marketing dollars.

Table 8.1 *Marketing activity log example as of end of March*

Activities / Target/Actual	J T/A	F T/A	M T/A	A T/A	M T/A	J T/A	J T/A	A T/A	S T/A	O T/A	N T/A	D T/A
Phone/e-mail one old contact per week	4/5	4/3	4/4	4/	4/	4/	4/	4/	4/	4/	4/	4/
Meet One-on-one network connection meetings	4/3	3/3	4/4	4/	5/	3/	3/	3/	4/	4/	4/	2/
Attend local networking events	5/4	4/6	5/6	4/	5/	3/	3/	3/	5/	5/	3/	3/
Make Cold calls/e-mail to potential prospects	20/18	20/20	20/25	20/	20/	20/	20/	20/	20/	20/	20/	20/
Identify new business prospects	8/9	8/7	8/6	8/	8/	8/	8/	8/	8/	8/	8/	8/
Meet with new business prospects	4/5	4/3	4/3	4/	4/	4/	4/	4/	4/	4/	4/	4/
Write proposals for potential clients	2/2	2/3	2/1	2/	2/	2/	2/	2/	2/	2/	2/	2/
Create new pieces of marketing content	2/0	2/2	2/2	2/	2/	2/	2/		2/	2/	2/	
Identify new potential business partner	1/3	1/0	1/0	1/	1/	1/	1/		1/	1/	1/	
Hold a marketing seminar or event			1/1						1/			

Numbers reflect monthly targets and actual number of tasks completed

Table 8.2 Sales activity log example for October and November

Sales Lead Follow Up			OS – Onsite visit		PC – Phone call		vm – voice mail		em – e-mail	
Warm Leads	Contact Name	Oct 02	Oct 09	Oct 16	Oct 23	Oct 30	Nov 06	Oct 13	Nov 20	Nov 27
1	Ford Motor Company	Bill Ford		em		PC		PC		
2	Al's Steel Manufacturing	Albert Smith		em						
3	Facebook	C.T. Winklevoss					em			
4	General Motors	Mary Berra		em						
5	McDonalds	Ronald McDuff							em	
6	Walt Disney Company	M.C. Mouse	vm							
7	~~Proctor & Gamble~~	~~Oral B. Tide~~				PC				
8	Intel	Gordon Moore			PC, em					
9	General Electric	Thomas Edison	em							
10	Johnson & Johnson	Ty Len Al	em		vm					
11	Nike	Phil Knight				em				
12	~~Caterpillar~~	~~B.L. Dozer~~		PC			vm/PC			

Tracks actual contacts with sales leads, types of contact, and closed or inactive leads.

These activity logs are for illustration purposes. You decide on the marketing and sales activities that are important for your business and the number of times each activity needs to occur. Set goals and try to meet them. Do not let good leads slip away without proper follow-up.

Branding

Every business needs to develop an image of how it wants to be perceived by the outside world. This is the *brand* it wants to convey to customers. What you want to be and your perspective customers' perceptions of what you are can end up as two different things. Are you an IT guy, a cybersecurity expert, or an Oracle database engineer?

Branding is about communicating with potential customers. You want to let them know why you are doing whatever it is you do. You need to make an emotional connection with your customers, and you need to differentiate yourself from your competition.

Your brand keeps you visible and increases mindshare with current and potential customers. This is particularly true for a lifestyle-minded consultant who may disappear from the scene every so often (e.g., spend winter in Florida). You want to be gone, but not forgotten.

One terrific way of doing this is to tell a story. Stories trigger different parts of the brain, and therefore, are more likely to be remembered. Come up with a story about how you helped a similar customer in the past. Try to add an element of emotion to the story whether it be humor or sadness, frustration, or joyful success. Describe a situation that is relevant to your immediate audience.

Another important aspect of branding is consistency. Whenever you are driving down the road and see golden arches, a yellow scallop shell or a green mermaid, you immediately think of McDonalds, Shell Oil, or Starbucks. The brand (and logo) is consistent. Your branding efforts should extend to all aspects of your business, including a business logo, your website, collateral material, and so on.

Branding starts with the name of your company. Research the business section of your state's website to make sure no one else has the name you are selecting. More importantly, make sure you can get the domain name associated with your business. You do not want to get all excited about your company name only to find out someone else already has the domain rights. If the domain name is available, the business name is probably available as well.

Secure your domain name. Your website is an important part of your branding efforts, and this name can become part of your e-mail address. To register a domain name, go to any of the domain registrars' websites. Look at two or three different sites. One may be offering special pricing at the time or different services you may find useful, such as e-mail accounts or website-building tools. Several popular registrars are Go Daddy, Register, Site Builder, and Wix. There are many others.

Coming up with a unique name is not easy. You can use your own name for the company, but that does not say much about what you do (and might not be available for John Smith). Many high-tech and biotech companies use made-up names or different spelling of existing names. One technique, called telescoping, is to take two words and mash them together to come up with an innovative word. Microchip and Software become Microsoft.

When I started my own consulting practice, I thought the name Field Consulting Services would be seen in different positive ways. Unfortunately, www.fieldconsulting.com was already taken. I settled for fieldconsulting.biz, which turned out to be a good conversation starter because very few other businesses used the .biz extension at that time. Last time I checked, the .com version was available for purchase for around $3,500, but I am already invested in the .biz brand. (I could buy the .com domain and have it point to the .biz website, but frankly, it is just not worth it to me.)

Two other essential elements of branding are a logo and a tagline. Both appear on my business card along with the standard contact information. Your logo helps to easily identify you and to differentiate you from others. Red and blue are the two most commonly used colors in logo design as they get a quick reaction from the eye and brain. Consider what your logo looks like printed from a black and white printer and as a small square on a social media site. Multi-colored logos can become a fuzzy image.

Your tagline should reflect either your services or your business values. I lean toward the business description because this provides a constant reminder to people of your services. Which of the following provides a clearer picture to you? "Securing Your Financial Future" or "Trusted for Generations." Both are actual taglines. They just convey different messages.

You want to have a tagline with some punch. Remember, you are trying to stand out in a crowd. A tagline of "Accounting Services" makes it clear what you do, but not how you differ from all others offering the same service. Check out what your competition is using for its tagline, logo, and business name. You want to be different. My tagline is "Optimizing Enterprise Software." It sounds generic to the general public, but has specific meaning to my target market.

My initial consulting firm provided a wide range of business skills, and we put together a complicated pocketed brochure with numerous inserts to reflect the business tools being presented to a specific client. A significant amount of money was spent on artwork, printing, and hiring a technical writer. I think more time went into developing the logo and brochure than we ever spent actually using them!

For my business, I designed my own simple logo and business card (which were inexpensively printed at Staples). My blue logo appears on my website, letterhead, invoices, and envelopes, the latter three I print on demand on my color printer. Additionally, I created a number of one-page collateral pieces (with my logo and tagline) highlighting various aspects of my business, which can be e-mailed to potential clients as PDF files or printed as necessary.

What you decide to do depends on your unique business. The materials required for someone providing accounting services are much different than for someone doing interior design. A logo and tagline are not something you need to get your business started; they just make it easier to market your services. Hold off on these until you are certain of your services. The wrong tagline adds little and perhaps, distracts from your actual business.

Once you have made up your mind, spend a little money and have someone develop a business logo for you. If done right, this should last the life of your business and be seen by all your business contacts. It is also a wise investment to get a professional headshot to include on your website or in your marketing material. A well-done studio photo has many uses from your LinkedIn or Facebook page to your website.

Collateral Material

Even a solopreneur consulting business needs to act and be professional; this means having the trappings of any other business, which includes business cards, a letterhead, and perhaps marketing collateral material. While none of this must be fancy or expensive, you may be living with some of your decisions for quite a while. A box or two of business cards can last for years.

Buy yourself a name tag. This helps to reinforce your brand, eliminates fussing at event sign-in tables, and separates you from others in a group. The nametag needs to include your name, your company name, logo (if you have one), or colors you have selected for your business (which can be the colors of your website for example).

If you participate in trade shows, including simple Chamber of Commerce events, you need additional materials. I had a banner professionally made for a table top display, but I have used that much less frequently than I expected. You want visitors to walk away with something to remember you. That can be a brochure, a flyer, or some sort of desktop trinket, but I would not spend a lot of money on this during your business startup.

One way to keep your costs down is to see if you can barter your services for the marketing help (logo design, headshots, etc.) you need. In addition to not having to pay as much, it potentially provides you with a referral customer you can use in the future.

At the end of the day, the key is to present yourself in the professional manner your prospects and potential customers are expecting.

Become an Expert

By getting people to think of you as an expert in your field, they are more likely to act as a sales channel for you and come to your website when they are thinking about the services you are offering. Becoming an expert is all about positioning, visibility, and credibility in the marketplace.

Writing articles is an excellent method of getting yourself in front of others and building credibility. Many publications, from magazines to blog sites, are all looking for good content. If the *Wall Street Journal* (or pick any other relevant publication) is willing to print your articles, then they must think you have something important to say. You do not need to be a national or international expert, but think about your geographic marketplace. Perhaps, a series of articles in the local press or a trade association publication might be just the trick.

Your challenge is to put together an informative piece that does not sound like a commercial and gets the reader to want to learn more about the topic. If you are having trouble thinking of an article that might appeal to your audience, think back on some of your successful engagements and present one or more of them as a case study. You may need to protect the name of your client or they may appreciate the publicity as well. Always check with the clients first before using their name or any potentially confidential information.

Getting exposure through articles helps in positioning yourself in the marketplace. You want to be seen as an expert resource for information in your subject area. One measure of your success is how often other people come to you for a quote or information for their articles. Being quoted by others further builds your position as a credible resource.

One added benefit is once you have published some articles, you can use the reprints (with proper permission) as marketing collateral pieces and on your own website.

Giving presentations at conferences and other public-speaking engagements (more on that later) helps to position you as an expert. Make sure you are presenting to potential clients or the influencers of potential clients.

Think about all the talking heads you see on TV these days. That is instant exposure and credibility for those people. Not everyone is suited for public appearances and interviews, so choose the tactics that are appropriate for you.

Developing articles, presentations, and speeches takes time. Content development is not something that most people should haphazardly throw together. Good content can last a lifetime and be repurposed as required. Each piece of information you create can take hours of time to develop. Unless you become one of a rare breed, do not expect compensation for your content. This is time spent on developing your image and building your own personal brand.

Digital Marketing

The Internet provides the means to communicate your message to large groups of people at a very affordable rate. Digital marketing encompasses social media activities, websites, and e-mail marketing. With so many digital marketing channels to choose from, it can seem overwhelming, and usage of the various social media tools changes over time. The influence of AOL, MySpace, and many others have come and gone.

Before engaging in a social media campaign, ask yourself the following questions:

Do your customers utilize this channel at all? If not, do not invest a lot of time or other resources on this.

When they utilize a tool, where are they in their purchasing process? If they are very early in the process, you need to generate a lot of leads. This requires a lot of work to move people through the process. You would like to attract them later in the buying process.

Do they come to the channel with a purchasing intent? If they come to the channel to exchange cat pictures with their friends, it is going to be difficult to engage with them.

Determine the two or three channels your customers are most likely to use and put your efforts there. If one channel declines in popularity, you still have other means of getting your message across. Determine what is commonly used within your industry and where you can differentiate yourself from your competition. If you have a B to C (business to consumer) model, Facebook and Instagram may be appropriate. If you have a B to B (business to business) model, LinkedIn or blogs may be a better avenue.

Drip marketing is the concept of reaching out to your contacts on a regular basis to stay in the front of their mind. This can be monthly e-mails, a periodic newsletter, or some other means of making contact on a regular basis. Coming up with something new to say every month is not easy unless creative writing is one of your skills. Fortunately, you do not need to create something new each time. See if you can find content from other people and send it out with a note about this interesting article you came across and thought they may want to read. Make sure to always give the original author credit for their work! Perhaps, you can even get one of your clients to contribute content that validates and endorses your services.

E-mail

It goes without saying that you need a business e-mail address and one that is separate from your personal e-mail. This way, your business e-mails are easier to track and you are not promoting snookems@abc.com to your customers. Having an address that ends in @gmail.com, @comcast.net, and so on is perfectly acceptable. But, if you have one tied into your website name, it presents a stronger message—steve@fieldconsulting.biz. That provides people with a memorable shortcut to your website. (This is also a requirement for setting up a LinkedIn business page.)

Equally important to your e-mail address is your list of e-mail contacts. This list has value; individuals have been sued for taking their company e-mail list to a competitor. Make sure you protect your list from hackers. Continue to add to your e-mail list over time and make sure it is up to date. This means replacing bounced e-mails with updated information whenever possible or dropping the bad e-mails from your list.

Your list helps you better target your social media and search advertising activities. You can upload your contact list to LinkedIn or Google, and they will create a list of lookalike customers with the same characteristics. This list is helpful in delivering your messages to the right people.

Constant Contact did a survey that showed 47 percent of recipients decide to open an e-mail based on the subject line. Think about how you react to unsolicited e-mails. Subject lines should be short, no more than 30 characters. When using e-mail for cold calling, make sure the content is concise, and any call for action shows up on a screen without scrolling.

The more targeted you can make your message, the better. The VP of Sales is probably not interested in the latest changes in OSHA safety standards.

Constant Contact, an e-mail marketing company, is one service that can assist in this process; others include Mail Chimp, FusionSoft, and Active Campaign. These services allow recipients to opt out of receiving your marketing messages. This feature is important to keep you in compliance with the CAN-SPAM Act, which sets the rules for mass commercial and promotional e-mailing. Violation of the act can be very expensive—over $40,000 per e-mail! Search the Internet for the CAN_SPAM Act to learn about the other easy-to-meet requirements.

Also, there are low-end Customer Relationship Management (CRM) software systems such as Hubspot, Odoo, and ACT. CRM software provides contact management, marketing, and sales tools in addition to e-mail support. Most of the services are cloud-based, starting with a free starter kit and pushing you toward a monthly subscription package. Check into a couple of these before making any long-term commitment as *the deals* are always changing.

Website

You need a website, period. Early on, your site is a means to provide credibility for your company. Once someone meets you, they can go to your website to learn more about you and your services. The unfortunate truth is a website can be all smoke and mirrors, which impresses the hell out of the viewer, but provides little real substance. You want your site to offer a taste of the services you provide without giving it away for free. Your site is a wonderful place to highlight customer references, which add to your credibility.

Your website should include the services you are offering, testimonials or references (if you have any), and a short bio on yourself. Some people do not even mention themselves on their website. They are trying to give the impression there is a larger organization in the background ready to support the customer. The downside is the truth comes out eventually, and it is never wise to start a relationship with deception.

A better approach is to reference your team of collaborators for the special projects. This should be a true statement. You continually cross paths with others who have skills outside your areas of expertise, and it is a useful idea to keep track of these people.

It is important your website encourages the capture of information about the site visitors. This can be as simple as their name and e-mail address. You need to have at least one lead magnet, or call to action, that gets them to give you this information. It should be for a fair exchange of value, and hopefully, they see it as a no brainer to sign up. They provide the data and you provide them something of substance. It can be a white paper, a subscription to your e-newsletter, a free service. You decide. Make sure you add the new e-mail names to your contact list.

Your call to action should be prominent on your homepage, but do not go overboard or it can make your site look tacky. If no one is providing their data, then your offering is not perceived as having value. Change your offering from time to time to see what attracts the most interest.

Search Engine Optimization (SEO) is a whole field of expertise dedicated on getting your website highly ranked in Google or Bing searches. It is worth talking to someone knowledgeable in this area to make sure your site is easy to find and has a decent Web ranking. If you have your site designed by a third party, make sure they consider how the site will be ranked by the search engines.

Paid Search Ads

Think about the user's intent. People on Facebook are doing many things other than buying business services. Facebook can play a role in your advertising campaign, but people searching the Internet using your keywords are much more likely to be active buyers. That is why, AdWords is such a success for Google. You can target a narrow geographic area and set a maximum on your daily spending limit. This can become expensive if you are attracting many non-relevant clicks. I do not want to be found by farmers looking for *field consulting*.

Find out where on the Internet your customers go to get purchasing information and where they are in the buying cycle when they access this information. Identify the searches where there is buying intent. Make sure your AdWords links take the viewer to a landing page on your website that provides the information they are seeking and the appropriate call to action. What you present should be different if they want education or if they are already looking to solicit quotes.

LinkedIn

LinkedIn is a very important tool to keep track of customers, potential customers, other consultants, and a variety of business professionals.

LinkedIn has over 150 million users in the United States alone and over 560 million worldwide. LinkedIn was developed for business people and enables you to build a network of quality contacts. You do not need to have a premium account, but there are advantages to do so (my business account allows me to send a limited number of e-mails to anyone on LinkedIn every month).

Some people try to build as large a network of contacts as possible. They link to anyone and everyone. My personal approach is to connect only if I have met the person, however briefly, at a networking event for example, or truly know the person as a friend, client, vendor, and so on. I want to be comfortable in being able to refer them to someone else. Having a very large number of LinkedIn contacts is only valuable if you are able to stay connected to them. Accepting random invites would dilute my networking pool and make it difficult to reconnect with those people. Even following those rules, anyone who has 10 or more years in business should be able to accumulate hundreds of contacts. My 900+ 1st degree contacts connect me to an additional 500,000+ people (2nd degree).

There is a balancing act between quantity and quality of connections. The law of large numbers suggests the more connections you have, the greater likelihood of success, but you also need to focus on quality. The value of LinkedIn builds over time as people you know move to different companies and provides a new way for you to get your foot in the door.

LinkedIn can provide you with visibility by entering group discussions or posting articles to demonstrate your expertise on certain topics. In addition to your personal account, you should also set up a LinkedIn business account at no additional cost. This allows you to promote your business as opposed to promoting yourself as an individual. Both can be important for different reasons (job hunting, for example).

Facebook

Facebook is another opportunity to consider, particularly if you are marketing and selling to the end consumer. B to B marketing on Facebook is still developing. Set up a separate Facebook account for your business to keep your personal life private. Even if you are a heavy Facebook user, the challenge is to make sure you keep the content current and relevant in your business account.

An important trend in business today is community-building. Getting your customers and prospective customers to interact on either your website or Facebook strengthens your business. You need to provide them with reasons to visit your page and start the interaction.

Instagram, now part of Facebook, is becoming more popular and allows you to put up pictures relevant to your business. This is very useful if your services have a visual focus and provides another opportunity to create community.

YouTube

A picture is worth a thousand words, so a video must be worth even more. Depending on the services you are offering, a video or series of videos can be very helpful as a marketing tool. You want to make sure they look professional, but that is not too difficult even using the video capability of today's smartphones. The finished products can be uploaded to YouTube and linked via your webpage or even included in an e-mail. Many people are using YouTube to generate a passive income stream to supplement their consulting or training services.

Podcasts

Podcasts are useful in telling an audio story. Again, it is important to convey the right image, so write out a script for your podcast and rehearse before you make the recording. Do not try to wing it. If you forget key points or go off topic and it sounds like you are just rambling.

Blogging

If you are a strong writer, blogging is a terrific way of showcasing that expertise. If writing is not your strong suit, there are still ways of coming up with useful content. Focus your blogs on your customers' problems and challenges. Address their pain points. Make sure your blog is tied to your domain. This helps to make your website easier to find for prospects looking for solutions like yours and helps to increase the search authority of your website (you rank higher on Google searches). Your blog becomes a keyword billboard for your website.

Blogs with guest posts, guest interviews, and client testimonials are all good ways to tap into other peoples' network of contacts.

If you do a blog, make sure to promote your posts via e-mail, LinkedIn, and other marketing channels to attract followers and casual viewers. You do not need to be posting every day or week, but it is good to have some continuity so that people might be looking forward to your next blog. You want to promote blog content and offers for prospects at all stages of the buying cycle—awareness, consideration, decision, and retention. Create a community that is attractive and provides value to those who participate and potential prospects.

E-Newsletter

Once you are comfortable with your ability to generate content (your own or from others), you can consider creating a newsletter that you send to your contact list. Services like TinyLetter (a division of MailChimp) simplify newsletter creation. All you need to do is come up with the content. Another resource to consider is paper.li, which allows you to gather articles from other sources and create your own newspaper. There is a free version as well as a *pro* version ($$), which provides more features, including an e-newsletter generator.

Unless you are sending these out on a regular basis, avoid using volume and issue numbers. They may only reflect how infrequently your newsletter comes out.

It is almost painful to mention, but make sure you proofread and run a spell check before you post any of your content for blogs, articles, or newsletters on the Internet. With today's tools, there is no excuse, except laziness, for putting out content with misspellings and poor grammar. That is not the impression you want to be leaving with the viewers.

Key Contacts

All of these tools are content-driven. You need to dedicate a certain amount of time to keep the content relevant, but do not become a slave to the technology. Marketing is important, but the time you spend on Facebook, Twitter, and other media is all time for which you are not getting paid.

You need to identify the *key contacts* in a company involved in the buying decision and understand how the buying process works for your potential customers.

Key contacts

The Final Approver. This is the person or team of people who make the final buy or no-buy decision. If the expenditure for your service is large, someone from senior management with the necessary spending authority will be part of the decision-making process. It would be great if you were interacting with them from day one, but they usually need confirming information from their own sources before you can get in the door.

The Influencer. This is a person who makes a recommendation to the Final Approver. Their task is to gather data confirming the decision. They add credibility to the decision. This person may not even work for the company. I have collected data and recommended service professionals for many of my clients.

The User. This is the person who ends up using your service, and in many cases, is the person getting the most benefit from the service. He or she may be the first to recognize the need for the service, might be the Influencer, but rarely has the authority to make the purchase.

One size does not fit all, and different marketing techniques may be necessary to reach the various contacts. Your sales tactics will also vary depending on the contact's role in the decision.

Back to the activity log. How many articles or blogs will you write each day or week? How many e-mails will you send out to prospective customers? How many videos will you create? The answer to any one of these can be none, but zero total marketing activity is not a good plan.

One tool used to improve manufacturing quality is called PDCA (Plan–Do–Check–Act), and it is just as appropriate for your marketing activities. You can have a great plan and be doing the activities, but you need to check or measure the impact of what you are doing. How many click-throughs does your e-mail campaign generate? How many people attend your event? If no one is visiting your website or reading your blogs or viewing your videos, what are you going to do? You need to figure out the right actions for this to change.

Before you do any marketing activities, determine how you can measure the success or failure of that activity. You should not expect thousands of responses for any one activity, but you should be getting some. What is your number for success? How will you measure it?

You do not have the resources to be doing things that do not work. Once you figure out what is working, double down on your time and energy in those areas until the returns diminish.

Start small by talking to your customers or potential customers without trying to sell. Find out all you can about their buying and decision-making process. Prototype your marketing efforts and get feedback before you commit full force. When you first start your business, you have plenty of time to dedicate to these activities, but once you are fulfilling the needs of your billable clients, your marketing time shrinks considerably.

Think about how you can leverage your activities. Perhaps, several blogs can become an article, an article can become a podcast, a podcast turns into a webinar, a webinar becomes a video, and so on. The ability to repurpose and leverage your content is important to save time and increase visibility.

Chapter 8: Homework
Update your notebook with the following:
- Create an activity log of your expected marketing efforts.
  o Determine your criteria for success and how to measure it.
- Secure a domain name.
  o Determine the name of your company.
- Decide what you need as far as a logo and tagline.
- Get business cards.
- Set up your website and e-mail.
- Create and organize your list of e-mail contacts.
- Determine what other collateral material your business needs.
  o Get it designed so you can print on demand.
- Set up appropriate social media accounts for your business.
- Determine how you can position yourself as an expert in your field.

CHAPTER 9

Networking

I've learned that people will forget what you said, people will forget what you did, but people will never forget how you made them feel.
—Maya Angelou

Marketing is about bringing potential clients to you. Networking is about your going out to find clients. Networking is face-to-face interactive marketing. It forces you out of your home office cocoon to meet and talk with other people. For most of us it is unusual to be able to find a viable client just by looking at a room full of people. Even when you cannot identify any prospects, the people in the room can still become a conduit to your potential customers. The best parts about networking are that anyone can do it and the costs can be kept very low.

Networking is like gardening. First you need to prepare the ground and sow the seeds, then you need to nurture the growth of your crops, and finally you get to reap the benefits of what you planted.

Here are some important guidelines to follow if you want to get the most out of your networking activities.

Preparing the Ground and Sowing the Seeds

A local networking expert continually emphasizes the need to set your goals or objectives before attending any networking event and come out of the activity with specific action items to follow up on after the event. Whom do you want to meet? How do you plan to follow up with them after the event? Collecting business cards to shove in a shoebox only results in a lot of stuffed shoeboxes.

When attending a "warm" networking event, where you have already met most of the attendees before, do you want to renew specific acquaintances? Are you looking for the few fresh faces in the room? I will approach someone who looks to be alone and introduce myself. They seem glad that someone is breaking the ice and taking an interest in them.

When attending a "cold" networking event, you might know very few people. Your approach might be to get as many business cards as possible, but fewer in depth contacts usually provide a better use of your time. Ask people about themselves and find out more than just what they do,

Follow-up is very important. Newly planted seeds die quickly without water. My first step is to connect to my new contacts on LinkedIn. If appropriate, I seek an introductory one-on-one meeting. Being timely is important. In the initial stages of getting to know someone, you are being measured on what you do. A quick response shows you are on top of your game.

Nowadays a hand-written note can rise above the e-mail clutter we all receive. This is particularly true if you are reaching high up into an organization.

The larger your network of contacts, the more likely you cross paths with someone who can help you meet your goals. This means your contacts need to be more than your close friends. Loose connections sometimes lead to new business opportunities. Diversity is important in a network. Push your boundaries in the types of networking activities you do. It gives you an unfamiliar perspective and provides access to people and ideas you have never had before.

I participate in a networking group that meets once a week for lunch on Thursdays. Most of the people who attend are interested in B to C opportunities and there are even a fair number of multi-level-marketing folks. This is not a forum my clients would ever attend. Nevertheless, I still need to eat lunch on Thursday and they meet close to my house. If I am not busy with a client or other value adding work, I attend the meetings. Recently I got two very strong leads—one was the wife of one of the regulars and another was a client of a new attendee. You never know the source of your next lead, so you need to keep yourself visible to as many people as time permits.

Nurturing the Crops

Very few of us live alone without human contact. You already have a network of people you know through schooling, your kid's activities, your religious affiliation, and so on. These are people who know you (perhaps only slightly) but might not know about the services your business offers.

Interactions with these people are usually in a more casual, minimal risk environment. Let them know what you are doing. Don't harass people but target a few who might be able to use your services or refer you to others. You need to start your business networking somewhere and you are already interacting with these people on a regular basis.

As a solo entrepreneur, you often feel you are out there looking for business on your own. You are not. Many other people just like you have their own specialized service offerings, perhaps overlapping with what you are doing or at least having clients in common. Get to know these people. I refer people I have met to my clients when I think there is a good fit. Referrals will come back to you as well.

If you want something from your network, you need to ask. People are generous and they want to help. Are you looking for an introduction to a certain person? Are you looking for someone with a certain skill set? Don't make your contacts guess what you need. I have attended many events where people stand up and say, "My need is..." Make sure you know "your ask" when you interact with your network. Listen to the needs of your contacts and be ready to assist them.

Make it easy for your network by staying in touch with them. Someone you friended on Facebook ten years ago may have a hard time remembering who you are. When they come across a potential lead, you want them to remember you.

Make sure you are easy to find. Once you have made a connection, make sure that person can easily find you. Is your LinkedIn e-mail up to date? Is your website one that is easy to remember?

Reconnect with old contacts. One suggestion is every day take a letter of the alphabet and pick a name to reconnect with. Keep your expectations low but see if you can strike up a conversation on common interest. If you cannot get a response, try again. If still nothing and the connection is not critical, let it go. Culling the herd is useful if it doesn't take much of your time.

One other idea is to tier your contacts. Assign attributes to each tier to help in knowing how to categorize your contacts. Tier 1 would be a close friend or someone you know you can count on. For me, my contacts at the various ERP software companies are my Tier 2 contacts. They are very important to me but not as critical as my Tier 1's. The following Tiers would be in descending order of importance. The unresponsive contact would fall into Tier 5 (scale of 1 to 5). Focus your time and energy on the higher tier contacts. General marketing e-mails go out to everyone, but time intensive activities (phone calls, face to face meetings, etc.) are concentrated on the higher tiers.

When you get an opportunity to reconnect, make sure you do your homework. Check out their LinkedIn profile to see what has changed since you last talked. Understand what you want out of the meeting. It is a promising idea to keep notes on each of your contacts. Review your notes to see what needs the other person had the last time you spoke.

Harvesting

Networking is a two-way street. Be on the lookout for ways that you can help your network, particularly those in your highest tiers. Respond quickly and accordingly to any referrals from your network. Follow through on any promises or commitments you make. One of my biggest disappointments is providing a lead to someone who doesn't follow up. I usually do not give them a second chance.

When you receive a lead that turns into actual business, let the referring party know and share your gratitude. If it is a major long-term contract, send them a holiday thank you present for as many years as the contract runs. This is a not a referral fee, but a thank you gift. A twenty-thousand-dollar contract is definitely worth a $50 restaurant gift card.

Even when the lead does not pan out, it is important to give feedback to your source. First, that shows them that you have followed up on the information they provided and second, they may have new information about the lead, such as employee turnover in the company, that may allow you to reengage at a later time.

Networking is not a passive activity. Networking is even more critical and time demanding for the sole practitioner consultant. You need to get out there and just do it. There are many ways to network and you need to find out what works best for you. Each activity takes time and this is usually unpaid time. You want to find activities where your time and money are best utilized. If you are finding certain activities to be a waste of your time and money, move on. There are many other opportunities.

Here are several popular networking methods. It is not necessary to engage in all of them and surely you can identify many more that fit your particular needs.

Public Speaking

This is an excellent way to both network and gain credibility for yourself. Just by being a speaker you are perceived by your audience to have a certain level of expertise. You want to find opportunities that allow you to present to potential customers or to others who might refer you to those customers. If you are uncomfortable doing this, start small, perhaps a local coffee gathering. Practice may not make you perfect but should help to overcome some of the anxiety of standing before a group of people. The people are there because they want to hear from you.

Make your presentation as fun and interactive as possible. Sometimes you must straight out lecture the audience, but the more engaged they are, the more attentive they become. Ask for a show of hands, ask questions of audience members, walk around. Find what works for you to create positive energy. You are the expert and they want to learn from you. In a best-case scenario, you may even get paid for speaking engagements. Few of us are this fortunate.

Start off by making sure you are comfortable talking in front of an audience. Take a public speaking class if necessary or join a Toastmaster group. You should feel very comfortable with the topic you are presenting and recognize that you know more about this topic than most of the audience.

Do not underestimate the time it takes to put together a good presentation. This can include a PowerPoint slide deck but make sure you proofread for grammar and spelling. You want to look professional and for goodness sake, avoid just reading from the slides! One benefit of putting in the work to create a really good presentation is you can repurpose parts of it over and over again for future needs.

Join an Organization

Figure out what organizations your customers belong to and those that connect you to your customers. Join a few of those. Look at the professional associations related to your service expertise. Finally, consider local community organizations such as your Chamber of Commerce or entrepreneurial forums. Each of these has a variety of meetings you can go to and meet other attendees.

Back in Chapter 4 you worked on describing your service offering in 25 words or less. Make sure you are well rehearsed because now you get to give your spiel when you meet new people. Remember, you are marketing at these meetings, not selling. You want to make sure you ask good questions to the people you meet. Demonstrate you are interested in them, not just yourself.

At one point I was attending five breakfasts, two luncheons and three or four evening events every month. You need to see which groups best meet your needs and focus your energy. The correct level is the one that allows you to make and nurture the right connections.

Once you determine which organizations are the best fit, you are ready to take the next step to further commit yourself to that group. This can range from volunteering for some of their activities all the way up to joining a board of directors. This is all non-billable time so plan accordingly. Even in a volunteer capacity, you still want to make sure you are communicating to others about the services you provide.

Meetup Groups

A wide range of networking groups already exists in your town and more are being formed all the time. The Meetup website defines a meetup as "neighbors getting together to learn something, do something, share something." Go to www.meetup.com to find a group that sparks your interest. Groups already exist, devoted to a wide range of interests including networking itself. You can even start your own group if you cannot find one that appeals to you.

These groups provide an excellent resource for the solopreneur. It is difficult not having peers to talk to about the problems your one-person operation is facing. These groups can fill that gap and provide excellent feedback.

Volunteer

During my career, I have served on the Board of Directors (unpaid positions) of several non-profit organizations. By doing so, I interacted with other board members on a regular basis and got to know quite a few people I might not have otherwise met. I currently serve on the Board of the New Enterprise Forum, an organization dedicated to helping entrepreneurs prepare their pitch for investors. The entrepreneurs are not my target audience but I enjoy the work and have come across other people through the organization that have provided me with business leads and advice.

Getting on a Board of Directors is just one example. Perhaps you are an architect. Volunteering for Habitat for Humanity building activities would put you in direct contact with builders in your community. I am sure there are numerous volunteer opportunities in your city related to your business services. Find one that aligns with your personal interests and ask how you can help. The key is you are able to get to know people on a sincere basis without the expectation that you are just there to hunt for customers.

Conferences

While not as popular as they once were, the right trade shows/conferences are a terrific way to network since they bring together a specific slice of the market. Focus on the ones that are correct for you. There are four ways you can take advantage of these events – by being an attendee, a speaker, an exhibitor, or a sponsor.

While exhibiting and sponsorship provide much greater exposure, the first two methods are much less expensive. Many conferences allow speakers to attend for free. You may need to pay for travel and lodgings but save hundreds of dollars in conference expense. Don't spend the big bucks to register for an entire show (unless you believe you get additional value for doing so), but instead consider getting an exhibit floor pass. These are often free or very affordable. A recent large manufacturing show had exhibit hall passes for $75 which included several keynote presentations, one conference session, and a lunch ticket.

One sponsoring opportunity that is sometimes inexpensive is to provide a delegate bag insert. Attendees generally receive a conference bag of collateral material and hopefully they look at your flyer at least once before pitching it. This is an opportune time to announce new services or include a press release. If you are reaching the right audience, some of them may eventually contact you. When going the sponsorship route, make sure you understand the benefits you will receive. Ask for the moon, it can't hurt. They will still want your money. Does your money buy you a list of attendees, a speaking opportunity, introductions to other speakers, or only promote your name to increase brand awareness?

The shows get you away from the normal day-to-day business activities and are an effective way of keeping current in your industry. You can see what competitors are doing and engage in some excellent interaction with vendors at the show. If you are bold enough, it is possible to mingle and network with other attendees.

Have you ever considered putting on your own conference? That may seem a bit ambitious but you are then perceived as the most important person involved with the event. What about starting with your own event listing you and another as speakers?

When I was in business school, I considered a career in brand management and interviewed with consumer product companies. During one such occasion, the job interviewer asked my opinion of a print ad that combined two completely different food products. The point was the ad attracted interest from users of each product and got them to think about using it with the other product. It created synergy. This same thing happens when you team up with another to put on a joint event. The marketing material goes to your mailing list as well as theirs.

I like to do speaking engagements with another complimentary speaker at events put on by a third-party organization such as a manufacturing association or a chamber of commerce. The third party does the heavy lifting to promote the event and the extra speaker makes the event attractive to a wider audience.

Many people today totally skip conferences so putting on your own virtual event can be a good substitute. Attracting an audience for a live webcast can be challenging but the program can be recorded and later available on-demand from your website. Furthermore, webcast attendees have no idea of the size of your audience, so they are not turned off by a low turnout.

Continuing Education

Here is a story told by my father (a lawyer) to a grandson entering the workforce:

> MIT Professor Edgerton was the inventor of high-speed photography using a strobe light to illuminate a speeding bullet meeting an object or a drop of water hitting a surface. He teamed up with other professors to form a small company researching and marketing this technology. When the U.S. government wanted a contractor to take pictures of the atomic bomb tests in the Pacific, Edgerton was selected. His small concern became EG&G, Inc., a publicly held New York Stock Exchange listed company dominating the field of high-speed photography.
>
> At some point early in my legal career, I remember asking him how EG&G managed to keep pace with others in a rapidly moving field of technology. His answer surprised me. He said that they would hire engineers with newly minted doctorate degrees, keep them in research work for 5 years and then either let them go or move them into marketing. He explained it was better for EG&G to keep hiring new engineers with the latest knowledge of the entire field than to try to keep the engineers already employed up to speed beyond their narrow area of research work.

Your field of expertise may not move with the speed of an atomic explosion but it does change and expand. The knowledge you have learned in your career continues to evolve. As a solopreneur it is all too easy to become isolated in the projects and work you are doing and lose touch with significant changes in your industry. It is imperative to keep current both in a general way and in your area of concentration.

This can be a win-win proposition. It is important to invest time (and money) in making sure you are keeping abreast of the trends and tools in your industry. Seminars, conferences, and formal training programs are all ways to achieve this while having exposure to a roomful of like-minded individuals. Use these opportunities to demonstrate your own credibility by asking intelligent questions during the program and to network with targeted individuals during the program breaks. Make sure you walk away with an attendance list with contact information.

Reading is one of the best ways to stay current and get exposure to new ideas. Your reading doesn't need to be all technical journals, although a few cannot hurt. As of this writing I am about two-thirds of the way through the biographies of every American president. That has nothing to do with manufacturing software but does provide many examples of good and bad leadership. I have included a list of books I have enjoyed or have been recommended to me in Appendix 1.

Listen to a Ted Talk. There are hundreds to choose from. While this does not help you meet anybody new, when you do, you will have gained some new insights to share with them.

Returning to the activity log, how many networking events do you want to attend each week? How many new organizations have you identified as worth joining? How many public speaking opportunities will you try to pursue? How many new leads do you want to generate each week or month?

A *More* magazine article[1] states that 79 percent of millionaires network at least five hours a month (I wonder how much they read?). I would be willing to bet most of them are not solopreneur consultants looking for work. That is just part of their standard practice. You should be able to do even better.

---

[1] *More* Magazine. April, 2015. "The 15 Habits of Rich People."

Chapter 9—Homework

Update your notebook with the following:

- Determine the types of networking events that are most promising for your business.
  o Find out where your customers "hang out"
  o You may need to attend several of them before finding the right fit
- Write down in your notebook what you want to achieve at each event.
  o Write down your post event follow-up plan
- Determine a way to stay connected with those you have met.
- Determine other means of networking with people outside of specific events.
- Keep your activity log up to date.

CHAPTER 10

Selling Your Services

For every sale you miss because you're too enthusiastic, you will miss a hundred because you're not enthusiastic enough. "Stop selling. Start helping."

—Zig Ziegler

So, by now, you have identified the value-adding services you want to sell, your potential customers, and a marketing scheme for getting the word out that you exist. Your next step is getting yourself ready to make a sale. Many excellent books have been written outlining the various steps in the sales process and how to do selling (see Appendix 1). Read a few of them to get ideas that work for you. Just remember, at the end of the day, most successful sales strategies are about establishing a relationship that builds value for the customer. It is about letting them know that you relate to their problems and can provide a welcome solution.

This chapter addresses getting yourself prepared for the sales conversation. A standard idiom is that sales is all about understanding your customer's pain and overcoming objections. To understand the objections, you need to know where the potential client falls in the sales cycle.

The buyer's journey travels from awareness of a problem to consideration of alternative solutions to the ultimate buying decision (some books and websites may list as many as seven or eight progressive steps). Your challenge is to determine at which stage you first want to be engaging with your potential clients. Engaging early means you have to educate the client. Education takes time and does not always bring in revenue. Engage too late and you may already be shut out of the options clients are willing to consider. Regardless of where you intend to engage, you want your selling process to align with their buying process, not to conflict with it.

Many companies try to attract highly qualified traffic to their website and automatically move the visitor through the early buying stages before human interaction even happens. After the education stage, customers need help in acknowledging and quantifying their pain points. How much is an old software system costing them in inefficiencies? How much could they lower their inventory investment? Once they are convinced they have a real problem, the next step is to lay out potential remedies to solve the issue. The last step is to help them over the hurdle of making the final decision. Perhaps, this is where you offer a discount or a foot-in-the-door teaser to help close the deal.

Understanding how your potential customers go about making their buying decision is critical for you in knowing when and how to engage with them and how to build a trusted relationship.

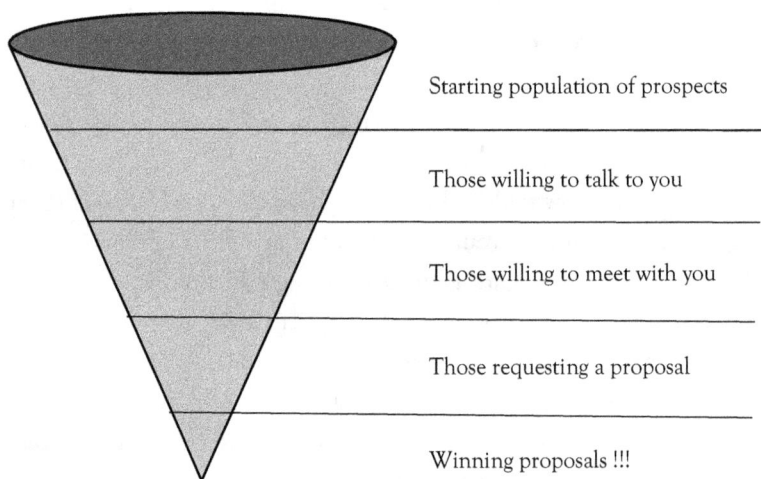

Starting population of prospects

Those willing to talk to you

Those willing to meet with you

Those requesting a proposal

Winning proposals !!!

Figure 10.1 Sales funnel

The sales funnel (Figure 10.1) is a well-recognized visual representation of how a large starting population of potential customers is winnowed down through a series of interactions until you are left with a much smaller number of real customers. For every XXX people or companies you go after, only a certain number of those lead to an initial interactive contact, fewer are willing to meet with you, and even fewer request you send them a proposal for your services. You need to figure out the starting number that provides you enough potential business at the tail end of the funnel. Your sales cycle is the time from your initial contact with a prospect to the point where you have a signed proposal.

Prospecting Lists

Hopefully, your marketing and networking activities generate enough prospects for you to be working through the sales funnel. Unfortunately, this does not work for everyone. Some people are just not any good at these functions and need to find another way of getting prospects.

Marketing firms exist that will sell you prospect lists. In my industry, many firms have a business model of posting software evaluations on the Internet to capture the e-mail addresses of those requesting the evaluations and then selling that information to software vendors and consultants. For a solopreneur, this can be expensive and buyer-beware. Some of these services are more reliable than others, but a good list is worth its price. You only need a small number of prospects to become customers to cover your expense, but you still need to put in the work to get those conversions.

Preparation

You come across potential clients in a variety of ways (via marketing, networking, referrals, etc.), and you want to be ready when those opportunities present themselves. You need to be prepared with what you want to say when face to face with a customer. Once you get past any introductory chit chat, you need to be able to quickly communicate to a client the value of your services and your personal credibility in delivering those services.

You do not know how much time a new prospect will provide you when you meet. You need to have everything from your *elevator pitch* (the less than two minutes time it takes to ride in an elevator) to a more in-depth dog and pony show. The key to the elevator pitch is to generate interest in your offering. You must be concise. You cannot get bogged down in unnecessary details or back story. You should practice and refine this pitch many times because this is the key starting point for many engagements.

When first getting started, try out several different introductory (less than 25 words) and elevator (two minute) pitches to see what feels the most comfortable and gets attention. Engineers are notorious for being all excited about their offering, but not being very good in explaining it to others. Make sure your offering is understandable in layman's terms.

The best result to expect from your introductory elevator pitch is the potential client's request to talk more later. Book a time and date. Be forward and request the meeting yourself if you believe it appropriate.

Understand the timing of your sales cycle. If you are selling a big-dollar project to a large corporation, it may take multiple meetings and months to close the deal. If you are selling a low-dollar quick assessment, the cycle should be much shorter. For the longer cycle, you need more preparation and more materials to support the effort.

Recognize the time and education required to make a potential client realize the benefit of what you are selling. Recently, I met a naturopathic doctor. I had no idea what that was or how that differed from a regular doctor. She had to spend time explaining to me about naturopathic medicine and how her services fit into the medical community. All of this was her time spent (wasted?) to educate me before she could even start to sell me on her services. Convincing people you have the best solution to a problem they have never heard about is a difficult selling process, but can also be very rewarding. Many high-tech companies are very successful doing just that.

Realize with whom who you are interacting; is it a user, an influencer, a decision maker? It is easy for me to convince an Inventory Manager that he or she needs a new ERP software system, but it is the CFO or Plant Manager who typically makes the buy decision. You can waste considerable time and opportunity if you are selling to the wrong person.

You may also need to prepare a more detailed presentation including examples of your work, your process, your success stories, and so on. That presentation can last from 30 to 60 minutes and should be designed in the format of a discussion more than a lecture. You want to be able to draw out the clients and better understand their issues and problems. During this discovery, you may find other opportunities to apply your services. By this time, you are generally pitching to higher ranking individuals in a company and you want to keep in mind the importance of their time. Do not waste it. Not all sales require this higher-level presentation, and your business may never need it, but it does not hurt to be prepared.

This is a situation where some people freeze. Standing up in front of a group of people and talking makes many people nervous. Appreciate that you know more about the subject matter than does your audience. This is your business, what you do for a living, and the reason they should hire you.

Come out of any meeting with a solid plan of next steps or action items. Will you be giving them a proposal? Do they need more information about your prior work? Is there a need for a follow-up meeting with different people? Think about the objections they have raised and if you have countered them all successfully.

These pitches take on aspects of a job interview. Preparation is critical. Practice what you are going to say until it becomes second nature. You want to know about the client, and they want to make sure you are the best candidate for the job they have in mind. Accepting the role of a solopreneur consultant means you are in for a lifetime of job interviews. The more prepared you are, the better the interview. Do your homework on the customer. With the amount of information available on the Internet today, there is no excuse for going in without basic knowledge of the company. A follow-up e-mail thanking them for their time can include additional information addressing their objections.

During a sales meeting, I like to give away small pieces of information that demonstrate my knowledge and provide the potential client with some value, but are teasers to the real services. I always leave the customer with a few handouts supporting my credibility and my processes. Hopefully, this keeps me on their radar whenever they think about their project.

Engagement

David Finkel, a respected business thinker and CEO of Maui Master-Mind, relates his five best techniques to improve a sales discussion:[1]

1. Magnify your prospects' pain and make the cost real to them and excruciating. Help them articulate the full cost of doing nothing. Useful questions to ask include:

   a. Tell me about your current situation.
   b. What's not working right now?

---

[1]   https://inc.com/david-finkel/the-5-most-powerful-sales-techniques.html

    c. What happens if you do not deal with this and find a solution?

    d. Why are you dealing with this now? (This can open the door to their true motivation.)

2. Create scarcity for your services and tap into the fear of loss. Nothing prompts action like the competitive urge. Find a way to inject competition into the conversation with prospects. Let them know you are a limited resource and can take on only a certain number of new clients each year. They need to commit soon if they want to get started this year.

3. Preempt sales objections. You probably hear the same objections repeatedly. Instead of letting objections come up and then having to overcome them, address and dissolve them before they are fully articulated by your prospects.

4. Save a key objection to the end and use that as a lever to close the sale. Close the objection and you close the sale. When you have a key objection, it makes sense to leave it to the end to use that objection to create the emotion and movement to close the deal.

5. Ask great questions that build customer motivation and restating and reframing your prospect's responses to help them sell themselves.

Getting Others to Sell for You

"When working you are not selling, while selling you are not working."
This is a challenge for every sole practitioner. Sales can be very time-consuming and the process itself does not provide very much income. On the other hand, while you are working with one client and making money, you cannot be selling to others at the same time. The key takeaway is you need to make sure you continue to devote time to selling. You cannot afford to let the pipeline run dry.

Learn to recognize which you enjoy more, the sales process or the delivery process. For sales people, it is all about the thrill of the hunt, of landing a client, or closing a big deal. The actual work is more of an afterthought. They may subcontract many of the tasks to others.

Other people are very uncomfortable with the sales process. Remember the earlier discussion on rejection? These people enjoy the nitty-gritty day-to-day work, but cannot stand the constant disappointment that is part of any sales effort. One solution to this dilemma is getting other people selling for you.

Why would someone else sell for you? The most obvious reason is they would get compensated for a successful sale. Websites have been set up to match service providers with clients while taking a piece of the action (some of these require you to submit a bid for the work). I never had much success with these sites, but I know others with a more positive experience. Sales representatives are individuals who would be glad to act as your sales team for a commission, but that removes you from the initial meeting with the client. They sell a variety of services and products to their network of clients.

One pitfall to avoid is getting hung up on revenue-sharing schemes with a third party long before there is any chance of having revenue. I can recall several occasions where an individual wanted to set up a complex contract on how we would compensate each other for referring work. After wasting time haggling about the contract, there was very little work ever shared.

My preferred model is to find individuals whom I refer work to and vice-versa. No *finder's fee* is involved. It will never be an exact exchange of business, but that does not matter.

At the 2015 University of Michigan Commencement Address, Paul Saginaw, one of the founders of Zingerman's, talked about the joy of giving. He said, "Just know that these things (material objects) don't bring joy like being generous does. Generosity leads to joy. It's simple and it's guaranteed. Generosity follows the natural law of the harvest. You reap more than you sow. When you give, you get back more."

This is true in the referral business world as well. The more you give, the more will come back to you. Some refer to this as the law of reciprocity. You have a client who has a need you cannot fulfill and you know someone who can do so. Both parties are thankful for the connection. Pass it along.

Another situation with mutual benefit is when you bring value to the referrer as well as the end client. This works when you find someone directly involved in your line of business that can recommend you.

In my practice, I know many of the vendors selling software. Their sales cycle is long and becomes more complicated if they must spend time educating their customer during the sales process. Their goal is to sell the software, pass the customer along to the implementation team, and move on to the next potential customer.

Part of my consulting role is to streamline the customer's acquisition process, educating them, and getting them to focus on their critical business issues and decision points. When it comes time to talk to the vendors, the discussions are on topic, quickly moving toward a final decision.

The vendors recommend me to companies looking for software. They know I am fair and unbiased in the evaluation process and get the customer ready to make an informed decision more quickly. I play fair with the vendors. I do not promise them any sales, but make sure they are included in the software review for any referral they provide to me.

Getting the Internet to Sell for You

The Internet is the first resource for many people looking for a product or service. It is important that you are easy to find. You want to use your website to attract business. You need to understand how to improve your website's visibility to search engines such as Google. Simply Google "How does Google rank websites" for a long list of sites with information that can help you do this.

It is a good idea to sign up for Google Analytics (http://google.com/analytics/). The free version helps you understand the volume of traffic to your website, time users spend on the site, and other useful metrics. Another useful site is Fastbase (https://analytics.fastbase.com). The Fastbase analytics provides more specific information on the individuals who have been visiting your site even if you do not buy the premium services.

In addition to simply having a website, you need to consider how you want people to engage with your business. As mentioned earlier, it is an excellent idea to figure out a means of capturing your Web visitor's names and e-mail addresses so that you can reach out to them for further engagement. You do not need to be devious about this, but make it a condition of being able to read or access certain content from your site. One example of this is a company called eTurboQuote. They offer a free software tool, but to download it, you need to provide your name, e-mail, and phone number. Many other examples can be found with a little exploring. Capturing the information is only the first step. You need to work these leads through your sales funnel.

Proposals

Your proposal can be a make-it or break-it moment in the sales process. Presenting your proposal in person is best because this allows you to explain the various aspects and answer any questions that come up. Frequently, proposals are e-mailed to potential clients. In either case, you want the proposal to clearly spell out the problem, your solution, and the fees for your services. Your proposal becomes your final and best sales tool. It needs to be clear and concise.

My client proposals have the following eight sections:

1. Executive Summary

   It is important the Executive Summary catches the attention of senior management. It needs to clearly state the problem and, at a high level, the work to be included in the project to solve the issues. Occasionally, senior management may decide not to read through a 20-page document and base their decision on the one-page summary. For that very reason, do not include pricing information in the summary.

2. Project Objectives

   Think of the project objectives as a stake in the ground. This is what the client is asking for at the time the proposal is written. Without this, the scope of the project can change dramatically with the client's expectation that you will do additional work for no additional money. This is also a measure of the expected results of the project. If the project meets or exceeds the objectives, it should be considered a success.

3. Project Benefits

   By listing the benefits of the project, the clients clearly understand the return they get from the investment in your services. These benefits can be *soft* rather than hard dollar numbers, but must be a true benefit to the client. For example, the ability to increase your client's customer satisfaction is a real benefit, but difficult to value.

4. Project Deliverables

The deliverables are the meat of the proposal: tasks to be done, work to be completed, and end results to be delivered to the client. If there are multiple project phases, this section should include the cost information for each phase.

5. Project Plan and Schedule

The schedule lets the client know how soon you can start the work and how long the work lasts. Sticking to the schedule is important for your client's view of the project's success. This is the section to include any resources you need from the client, including the time commitment from certain individuals in the company. You don't want to be held to a fixed schedule if they cannot provide the necessary resources.

6. Project Fees and Payment Schedule

The section on fees and payments needs to clearly outline the amount to be billed, when billings occur, and when payment is expected. I have billed at the completion of a project phase and on a monthly basis. Phased billing is done on my fixed-fee proposals, and monthly billing when I am working at an hourly rate.

7. Project Administration

The administration section includes all your contact information, the time for which the proposal is valid (30, 60, 90 days), and a signature page for written approval of the proposal. Leaving the proposal open for a longer period might lock you into certain work after you have already accepted other work in the same time period.

8. Appendix of Terms and Conditions

I have created standard terms and conditions that I attach to every proposal as an appendix. These terms and conditions are an attempt to limit my liability in case of a disgruntled client and to indicate where any legal action takes place (near me, not necessarily near my client). Fortunately, I have never had to test whether these terms and conditions actually stand up in court.

A copy of my terms and conditions is included in Appendix 4 of this book plus one other that I received from an environmental testing company. You can see the similarity and differences between the two. These highlight the need to have terms and conditions appropriate for your business and provide an excellent time to re-engage with an attorney. Once set, your terms should be good for quite a while.

One other section to consider including would relate to out-of-scope activities. I help companies select software, I want nothing to do with the hardware selection, configuration, and installation. Even if there are other tasks I would be willing to do, I might list them as out-of-scope to make sure the client understands those activities are not covered under the project proposal.

Chapter 10: Homework
Update your notebook with the following:
- Perfect your introductory and elevator pitches.
- Prepare longer PowerPoint (or verbal) presentations.
- Determine how you can get others to be selling for you.
  o Determine what you are willing to pay for sales referrals.
- Mock up a draft proposal. Most of this should be boiler-plate that you can use with multiple potential clients. By doing this now, you will have a much faster turnaround time for submitting real proposals.
- Check with your lawyer on the terms and conditions for your proposals.

CHAPTER 11

Managing Subcontractors and Partnerships

Coming together is a beginning; keeping together is progress; working together is success.

—Henry Ford

In the early 2000s, the State of Michigan provided training money to help companies develop the skills of their workforce. In response, I developed training courses covering various aspects of traditional inventory and production control. One client absorbed my full curriculum and was looking for additional training on lean manufacturing. I know a lot about lean manufacturing, but that is not my core expertise.

I turned to Curtis, someone who had worked for me in the past and brought him into this client. What started as a subcontract arrangement quickly shifted to a partnership where we each had input on the project deliverables. The end result was more than a year of additional work for both of us.

Subcontractors

Subcontractors can be a godsend to help alleviate work overload or to provide skills outside your standard practice, but these engagements need to be carefully managed. When you introduce a subcontractor to your client, there is guilt by association. It they do a respectable job, you get partial credit. When they do not, you may get all the blame.

The first step is to consider if the subcontractor is someone you would have work for you. I had hired Curtis when I worked for a larger consulting organization and had full confidence in his skill set. Another time I turned down the opportunity to bring in someone on a job because

I was not comfortable on how I would be represented. You need to be confident in their abilities.

It is important to have a signed contract with any subcontractor who is working for you. This provides certain protections and helps establish the business relationship. (See sample Subcontractor Agreement in Appendix 2.) The following items need to be addressed in the contract:

1. Independent contractor
   The IRS is on the lookout for people being called independent contractors when they are really employees. Certain rules, including overtime pay, apply to employees but not independent contractors. You want to make it very clear that these people are not your employees.

2. Intellectual property rights
   During the project, certain intellectual property might be developed such as training materials, research data, etc. Who is going to own this material once the project is done? Who has rights to use it again in the future? While there is no one right answer, you want to address these issues before the project starts.

3. Confidentiality
   Your client may require you to sign a non-disclosure agreement (I encounter this on almost all of my projects), and you need to make sure anyone working under your authority follow the same rules. Additionally, you may have your own proprietary information that you expose to the subcontractors, but you do not want them to share with others.

4. Client ownership
   Make sure your client stays your client (at least as long as you want them). I have seen certain instances where a subcontractor has taken over client management duties and, in one case, had the consultant kicked out. You need to be the one reporting to senior management on the progress of the project. You do the invoicing. You do the proposal renegotiations.

5. Pay
   A subcontractor is doing work for you, not for the client. You continue to bill the client and receive money. Your subcontractor is then

paid by you. Therefore, it is very important to state the amount to be paid and the timing of the payments. If your client is slow in paying you, will you have the cash to pay your subcontractor? If not, will the subcontractor continue to work for you? Spelling this out upfront in a contract heads off future problems. Also consider the out-of-pocket expenses that might be incurred by the subcontractor. Make sure everyone understands what is an acceptable expense and what prior authorizations might be required.

Partnerships

Subcontractors are subordinate to you. They work for you. Partnerships are a more level playing field. Each party has something to add to the client's success. Depending on the situation, each of you may be billing the client separately and negotiating separately. The key is the work you are doing needs to mesh with that of your partners. You need to work together.

Many of my partnerships started without having any clients, but realizing our skills were complimentary and added value to a potential client. A less formal proposal or written document is still a sound idea to protect your intellectual assets and highlight who has what responsibilities and when certain tasks need to be done (see Appendix 3 for a sample non-disclosure agreement that could be used with partners). As an example, I have partners who focus on installing hardware while my concentration is on the software side of the business. They do their thing and I do mine. We coordinate certain activities, but each of us contracts directly with the client.

Partnerships require ongoing communication. You need to be talking with your partners outside of client engagements to discuss any issues needing to be resolved between your two parties. Every week I speak with one of my business partners regardless of our current level of joint client activity. We can always find new prospecting or marketing ideas to discuss.

I want partners I trust, know will be professional, and get their job done on schedule. I may recommend them to a client, but how they do their work (and get paid) is entirely up to them.

Chapter 11: Homework
Update your notebook with the following:
- Determine if you want to use subcontractors or partners (it is not required!).
- If yes,
    o Figure out who you might use and for what situation.
    o Rough out a subcontractor agreement if warranted.
    o Rough out a non-disclosure agreement if warranted.
    o Determine a pattern for communication.

PART IV

What They Do Not Teach You in Business School

CHAPTER 12

Odds and Ends and Insurance

I had no idea of the character. But the moment I was dressed, the clothes and the make-up made me feel the person he was. I began to know him, and by the time I walked onto the stage he was fully born.
—Charlie Chaplin

Appearance and Dress Code

My German business mentor back in the late 1970s was upset with my choice of car—a Buick Opel made in Europe. In no uncertain terms, he let me know my next car better be American made. It was all about appearances when I would travel to customers and vendors. (To this day, I have never owned a Ford, GM, or Chrysler vehicle. On the other hand, I have never had any of them or any large Tier-1 auto supplier as a client.)

Your appearance adds to your credibility and your value. By looking professional (and driving the right car), you are construed as someone who must be successful, good at what you do, and other people are paying you well for your services. You convey a certain image to your public and to yourself.

I might start early morning work at my home office wearing not much more than a sweat suit or bathrobe and slippers. I even hold client and networking phone conversations dressed that way (particularly if I plan on exercising after the phone call). Out of the house and meeting clients, my appearance tells a different story.

While society's dress code has become more casual over the years, a good rule of thumb for first contact is to match the appearance of the most dressed up person you will be meeting. I work with many manufacturing company employees, from the oil-stained shop workers right up to the president of the organization. Appearance is important. I want to be perceived on the same level as the president. If my first meeting is with a small company plant manager, I do not need to make as much of a fashion statement.

Software developers have an image of blue jeans and t-shirts, but the more successful ones still visually display their success (expensive watch, etc.). Even Facebook's Mark Zuckerberg ditched his hoodie look to appear more professional to the investment community.

Once a new client engagement is underway, you can see how the people in the organization dress and modify your own if you wish, but always remain at the top end of the scale. Some consultants wear an expensive suit and tie, no matter with whom they work. It is part of their image of success.

A final note on appearance and technology. Nowadays, Internet video meetings through Skype and other comparable products are very common. The parties at the other end of the call not only see you, but also see a background. You want to look professional and you want your background to do the same. A background of the kitchen sink or the children's toys sends a much different message than a bookcase or an office-looking environment. This only needs to be temporary setup for the duration of the call, so test a few different setups until you find one where you are satisfied.

Office Space

When your business is just getting started, think about where you interact with your customers. Do you need to have an office for them to visit or do you see them at their place of work? Can you meet with them in a neutral third-party environment?

Renting an office, furnishing it, installing a phone and the Internet are all upfront expenses with no immediate return. My initial consulting partnership (the one with the fancy brochures) rented office space, half of which was always empty. We picked up second-hand furniture and had to buy and install a computer network to share information.

None of that produced any real income, yet created a monthly expense. Our larger clients never came to the office, and those visitors that might have been impressed were never going to amount to significant income.

One option gaining in popularity is co-working spaces with companies such as WeWork or Office Evolution, which are setting up locations across the United States and even around the world. The premise is to create a community of independent workers who pay a *membership* fee for access to shared working space and office amenities such as high-speed Internet, printers, and a kitchenette. The workers can be in different businesses and have minimal interaction outside of sharing space. This is a less expensive alternative to renting office space and does not require year-long leases. At the time of writing this book, co-working spaces in Southeast Michigan ranged from $290 to $600 per month for full any-time access.

Many very successful consultants work out of their home (or even their car!). The downside to a home office is the household interruptions and the distractions that keep you from doing your work. Can you talk on the phone without the dog barking or the baby crying in the background? I am amazed how many calls I take where that is actually happening on the other end of the line.

Start with the home office and see how it works. If you cannot get any work done, look for business incubator space. Some consultants need an office, but see if you can get by without one. I meet almost all of my customers at their facility and many networking clients at the local Panera Bread or Starbucks. Those places have become favorite hangouts for many solopreneurs. I spoke with an architect from a one-man firm who designs residential homes. For him, it was critical to have his own office space where potential customers could see examples of his prior work and talk to him about their own needs. Every business is different.

Personal Insurance

Leaving a larger company to go out on your own eliminates certain personal insurance coverage. If you are fortunate, your family may be covered by a spouse's plan. If not, health insurance is coverage you cannot overlook. The risks are simply too high.

Even under the Affordable Care Act (Obamacare), finding affordable health insurance is a real challenge. Many people join chambers of commerce or similar organizations to take advantage of their member insurance programs, but the insurance companies cut way back on those in recent years. Shop around to find the best alternative for your situation.

Each state is managing the health insurance issue slightly differently, and you should be able to easily find your state's information on the Internet. Note that most non-corporate health insurance plans do not provide routine dental or vision insurance. If it looks like your children need orthodontic work, dental insurance might be a smart addition (beware of your plan's orthodontic limits).

One other vehicle you should consider is the use of a Health Savings Account (HSA). This allows you to set aside pre-tax money every year (up to $7,100 for a family in 2020) to be used for medical expenses. Unused money is rolled over into future years for your use while earning value over time. You need to have the right kind of health insurance (high deductible) and enough income to be able to afford setting aside this money for future spending. Check out IRS Publication 969 for details on HSAs and whether you qualify (or talk to your accountant).

Other insurance such as life insurance and disability coverage are an individual decision, but recognize you have probably lost any coverage provided by your former employer.

Business Insurance

You may also require commercial insurance. The four major types of policies to consider are premise liability, workers compensation, professional liability, and auto.

If your office is in your home and your customers come to your office, your homeowner's policy may not provide liability coverage if something was to happen to them on your property (e.g., slip on your un-shoveled sidewalk). your homeowner's policy may provide some allowance, but it can be very limited. Once your home business activity is significant, you should investigate getting a second business-policy from the same insurance company. This avoids conflicts between the two policies. If you work out of a home office but never have visitors, a business policy is really not necessary unless your business assets exceed what might be covered under your homeowner's policy in the event of loss. That $15,000 graphic design computer and printer might not be covered by your homeowner's policy.

If you rent space outside your home, your homeowner's policy does not apply at all. Make sure your get commercial liability package. Hey, if you can afford to rent office space, you can afford the insurance.

A few clients have requested a copy of my workers compensation insurance if I was doing work for them in a factory or field location. I have never bothered to get this type of insurance (it is required if you have employees) but have had to negotiate around this with the client. Understand your own potential needs in this area and talk to your agent.

As a consultant or service provider, you provide advice and services to your client. They follow your advice, and the results are not always predictable. Are you responsible? Can they sue you? Even if the first answer is negative, you can still be sued. Professional liability insurance, commonly known as errors and omissions (E&O) insurance, protects you in the event a customer sues you for providing bad or damaging service. If, as a home hair stylist, you caused a client's hair to fall out, or if, as a graphic artist, you mistakenly put the wrong sales price in an ad, you can be sued.

You need to consider the risks you face for the services you provide. If the risks are significant, then E&O insurance is a smart move. I have never purchased E&O insurance and try to reduce my personal risk by including a clause in my client contracts limiting damages to the amount I was paid by the customer. Fortunately, I have never had to test whether this was adequate. Another method is to minimize the business assets that would be vulnerable in a law suit. Do not keep hundreds of thousands of dollars in your business checking account. If your business assets consist of several hundred dollars in a checking account and an old $1,000 computer, your present-day liability is minimal.

Last, but not least, there is auto insurance. The test for whether you need commercial coverage is threefold. First, how is the vehicle titled? If it is in the name of your business, then you need commercial coverage. Secondly, how is the vehicle being used? If you are carrying product samples, tools, or equipment needed for your business, then once again commercial insurance is needed. If you drive around in a box truck to haul furniture for your moving business, that is pretty clearly a commercial use of the vehicle. If your business name is permanently affixed to the vehicle, once again that indicates commercial use. Finally, there is the question of how exclusively the vehicle is being used for business. If used primarily for business driving, commercial insurance is probably needed. Many personal auto policies exclude driving for business, although you can add an endorsement to allow it.

Most of us only have murky answers to these insurance questions. Check with an insurance agent to get a better understanding of your unique needs.

Chapter 12: Homework
Update your notebook (as appropriate) with the following:
- Make sure your work wardrobe is adequate.
- Determine what you need to do as far as office space.
- Determine what you need to do regarding insurance.
  o Health
    o Determine if you can take advantage of a Health Savings Account.
  o Liability
  o Workers compensation
  o Auto
  o Life
  o Disability
  o Other

CHAPTER 13

Ethics

Integrity is not a conditional word. It doesn't blow in the wind or change with the weather. It is the inner image of yourself, and if you look in there and see a man who won't cheat, then you know he never will.
— John MacDonald in *The Turquoise Lament*

Always do right. This will gratify some people and astonish the rest.
— Mark Twain

As a one-person service organization, you are constantly selling yourself, your credibility, and your professionalism. You do not want to do anything to put that in jeopardy. With the Internet and social media, the business world today is a small place, and you do not want to participate in any actions that damage your reputation.

You want to believe you know the difference between taking the right actions versus the wrong actions in particular circumstances, but in the business world, there are a number of areas in various shades of gray. The first step is to know when you are entering a gray area. And, there will be temptations.

Referral Fees

A number of honest vendors exist who might offer you a referral fee if you can get them in the door of your client. Some may even provide a benefit to your client. On the flip side, unscrupulous vendors also offer referral fees, but end up costing your client far more than any benefit they receive.

Unfortunately, there is no safe way of guaranteeing which category a vendor falls under. You need to avoid even the appearance of any connection between you and the second type of vendor.

A related category is working with other consultants. Your area of expertise cannot cover all of the areas where your client needs help and you may wish to bring in other resources. Other consultants may call on you from time to time.

Some people ask for a piece of the action for bringing in the extra resource. I shy away from that. If I had work for another person, I might recommend them, but it is their job to negotiate with the client. My philosophy is what goes around comes around. If I am getting work for others, they will look for work for me.

Refusing any sort of referral fees may cost you a few dollars short term, but can make life much easier in the long run.

Conflicts of Interest

A second issue is conflicts of interest. You need to be able to identify those or any perceptions of a conflict. Examples might be where you are doing work for one client and bring them in as a vendor for a second client. Are you serving client #1 or client #2? It is possible to serve both, but you need to make sure everyone understands your position with each entity.

Another example of a gray area is accepting clients who compete in the same business. If your expertise is pure website design, you might be able to reconcile doing design work for both companies if the end results are totally different. I would interpret using the same design for both as a conflict of interest. A more obvious conflict would be attempting to create an overall marketing strategy for both.

Another conflict of interest you may come across occurs when a third party brings you in to work with a client where they are also engaged. You may deal directly with the client for your work, but the third party is making suggestions to the client that you do not feel are appropriate.

A contractor recommended an architect to a young couple building a house. While the architect was doing his design work, the contractor was trying to get the couple to add additional features the architect thought were costly and not necessary. Should the architect have told the couple his opinion but risk angering the contractor? In this case, he kept his mouth shut. Perhaps a better alternative would have been to express his opinion directly to the contractor, but that also has risk.

Ask yourself if your actions are in the best interest of the client. If not, you have a conflict that needs to be addressed.

Conflicts of Morals

You are the boss. You decide with whom you want to work. Would you do work for a Donald Trump re-election campaign? What about a Bernie Sander's election campaign? Planned Parenthood? Right-To-Life? Hey Michigan fans, would you accept computer programming work that improves Ohio State football recruitment performance (or vice-versa)? What if you were offered $100,000 for three months of work? What if it is the only work you have been offered in six months?

It is not always an easy decision. You do not need to accept every potential client, but you do need to do your best work for any client you accept. Take a few minutes and think about situations you might come across where your personal beliefs are so strong (if any) that you would not want the client engagement. Determine how you plan to respond and write it down in your notebook. It will help make your actions easier if you ever confront this situation.

Confidentiality

Related to the conflict of interest point, maintaining the confidentiality of information learned at a client is paramount. This can be anything from business plans to hiring or firing information to the opinions of certain people about other people. Disclosure of this information can be hurtful to your client and its employees. For that matter, it can even be criminal if you are working for a publicly held business.

This means more than just keeping silent. You need to take steps to make sure your client's information is not leaked by someone hacking or stealing your computer or briefcase. Try to leave all critical client information at the company between your visits. This is not always possible (if you need to work offsite), but minimizes your exposure.

Attempting Unqualified Work

Another ethical area is taking on work you really are not qualified to do. You may have a customer who loves the services you are providing and asks for something new. If that falls within your expertise, great. If not, resist the temptation of a few extra dollars, and find someone who really knows that area.

As an example, many of my manufacturing clients are interested in the practice of lean manufacturing as an add-on to the process improvement services I provide. I understand lean manufacturing principles and can talk the lean talk, but there are many individuals whose expertise far exceeds mine and would be better consultants in that area. By bringing in one of these experts, perhaps someday that expert will recommend me to someone they know needing a new software system.

An offshoot of this is being able to identify a project that is just not working and be willing to end the project rather than *milking it* for some period. I had a client who treated his employees like mushrooms—kept them in the dark covered in crap. This was a forging facility, a notoriously filthy place to start with. I tried various means to help them clean up their operation so that the employees could see what they were doing and find the needed tooling and fixtures. The problem was the business owner was not going to change his attitude and did not think making the workplace easier for the employees was important. I wished them all the best and walked away from that assignment.

Bill Padding

Many people end up billing the customer for time spent on a project. Make sure you keep an accurate record of your time and how that time was spent so that you can report the detail behind a summary invoice if requested. Padding the bill may provide a short-term benefit, but you risk ruining your name, gaining a reputation for being overpriced, and destroying long-term possibilities.

At the end of the day, it does not matter whether you think you are on the right side of an ethical issue. It matters what the customer thinks. Their perception is your realty.

Steve Reitmeister of Zack's Investment Research recently wrote "Work hard … but always play fair. There is no monetary amount worth even a momentary lapse in ethics. That includes putting the clients concerns ahead of your own. Right is right and that's the end of the discussion." That says it all.

It's a Small World

Back in the 1980s, I was sent to Singapore to help my company move production operations overseas. I left my three-year-old and five-month-old sons with my wife, so, of course, I had to find presents to bring back for all three of them. My wife's gift was easy, but I had a harder time finding something for the boys. I finally found a Toys "R" Us store and located appropriate gifts. (Interestingly, the world map puzzles all had Singapore in the center of the map instead of the United States.) This was my lightbulb flash of recognition of the global market we now all live. Any product can be sourced and found almost anywhere in the world.

Bringing this closer to home, I have spent most of my employed career working in Michigan. I still run into people I worked with 30 years ago. The manufacturing business world is just not that large, and I am sure the same can be said for whatever industry you come from.

Nowadays, it is all too easy to be publicly critical of your former employers. However, there is little to be gained and much that can be sacrificed. It really is a small world, and you only have one reputation.

Be careful not to burn bridges throughout your working years. I have been laid off by several companies during my career, but always parted in good graces. This has resulted in tens of thousands of dollars of later consulting income from some of those very same companies. In fact, I was more highly paid as a consultant than as an employee! See each work experience as an opportunity to build your credentials and your network.

Chapter 13: Homework
Update your notebook with the following:
- Try to identify potential areas of conflict in your business.
- Try to identify where you would draw the line with regard to moral issues you might come across with your potential clients.
- Determine how you will address these issues when they arise.
  o Write it down so you can refer to it at a later time.

CHAPTER 14

The Dangers of Success and Failure

Success is not final; failure is not fatal; it is the courage to continue that counts.

—Winston Churchill

It's failure that gives you the proper perspective on success.

—Ellen DeGeneres

People choose a lifestyle business for the freedom it provides them. Both success and failure can impose a burden on that freedom.

Danger of Success: Landing a Sugar Daddy

It is common for a start-up consultant to land an initial large client who demands much of their time and pays them well for their services. This can happen if you have recently left a company and they still need your services. That is how I first got started doing consulting. It can also happen if you have a friend or relative who needs your help and learns of your availability (although they may not pay as well!).

The danger is you become complacent with that client and are not out looking for other work. No matter how large the assignment, the day will come when you are no longer required and you need to make sure there is other work in your pipeline. The alternative is to go through long valleys of time without work or income before you head back up a mountain of riches. This is easier for some people than others, but creates more stress for your family. Bills need to be paid every month, regardless of whether you have billable time or not that month.

Danger of Success: More Work than You Can Handle

One pattern you slip into when working for yourself is to never say no to the right kind of business projects that fit your service profile. Business does not always arrive in a nice steady stream, but comes in peaks and valleys. If you are lucky, you can tell your customers they must wait until you finish other jobs. That does not work for most people (or companies) as the customer can find other resources.

The result is the work can become overwhelming at some point. You need to be prepared for this and figure out how to expand your capacity. You can hire people, but now you no longer have a lifestyle business. That is fine if you are agreeable and accept that.

Another option is to find others who can do the work as your subcontractor. They can fill in when needed, but you are not committed to keep them busy all of the time.

A third option is to increase the number of hours you are working to get everything done. While that might work in the short term, working 80 hours a week is probably not the lifestyle you were looking for.

The final option is to learn to say no. Customers may be prepared to wait for you to have an opening if your services are really that special and in high demand. If not, you have lost some business, but maintained your lifestyle.

Danger of Success: Work Offered Outside Area of Focus

It is easy to say yes when offered work outside your area of focus. Every business encounters dry spells, and it is tempting to accept work that falls outside of your normal services. If properly managed, this can be a good occurrence. It may expose you to new ideas and provide you with new skills you might not pick up any other way. It also pays the bills.

The danger in accepting work that does fit your business plan is you might be taking on lower-paying jobs or getting yourself into areas where you do not have the technical competence to do the work in an efficient manner. This can result in spending unpaid hours finishing up certain tasks, which is the same as accepting lower fees.

Balance the trade-off of getting into new areas of knowledge with working for less money. Gaining new capabilities while maintaining your fee structure is a win–win situation—as long as you enjoy the new work experiences.

Be careful not to get in over your head. You may be an expert on financial report writing, but that does not necessarily mean you know how to put together a budget. Similar areas but different skillsets are required.

If you ever find yourself in over your head, best to admit it and extract yourself from the situation. I had a client who needed help integrating his online store with his accounting system. I spent 8 to 10 hours working on this before realizing this was beyond my skillset. I admitted I could not help him and did not charge him for my time spent. I also provided the name of a resource that could assist him. Cut your losses and move on to the next job.

Danger of Success: Enjoying the Lifestyle Too Much

It is possible to get carried away with the freedom of working when you want to and for whom you want to. However, it can be very challenging to turn the work off and back on again. You need to do everything with a purpose. When you do not need to answer to anyone else, it is important to create your own structure. You need to set up routines within your work week to keep you focused on the tasks that need to be accomplished. Self-discipline is not always easy.

If you become unavailable for long periods (that trip around the world), your customers may lose track of you and find alternative solutions. When you return to business, the customers may not be there and you have to start from scratch. This is a balancing act. You need to find the right mix of work and free time.

Learning from Failure: Pulling the Plug

Many people try to become solopreneur consultants and fail. Failure in certain areas (high tech, for example) is seen as a badge of honor, but it is unlikely anyone financially dependent on you views this the same way. If your objective is to spend more time with your loved ones, you do not want to use that time fighting about your lack of income. This is why, it is so important everyone in your family understands what you are trying to do and how to measure success and failure.

You need to be able to recognize when your plans and goals are not achievable and be able to pull the plug on your consulting practice. Failure can provide some important lessons. Was there serious interest in the services you were selling? Were you able to present yourself and meet the right people through networking?

My first foray into consulting was not a great success. My wife considers it a failure (and she is right). While it allowed me to spend more time with my young kids, it did not bring in sufficient income to support the family. I initially managed to find a few good clients (thank you Somanetics and Zingerman's!!), but just not enough, and there was no consistency. I finally pulled the plug and took a salaried consulting position with a larger organization.

While failure is a harsh instructor, I learned much from this experience: the impact of sporadic income on my family and the need to focus on my areas of expertise. The salaried consulting position provided exactly that. Making the change allowed me to sell production management services (my expertise) to small- and mid-sized manufacturers.

Through my initial consulting foray, I picked up new skill sets that have served me well in my current consulting practice. I learned much more about networking a room full of people. I learned how to manage clients. I learned how to put together budgets and cashflow statements. I learned there was no reason for me to invest in a real office because none of my ideal clients would ever be visiting me. None of that would have happened without the failed endeavor. Use your failures wisely, and some day, you will get a second chance at a solopreneur consulting opportunity.

Chapter 14: Homework

Update your notebook with the following:

- Determine how much time you want to devote to your business.
    - o Also, determine how much time you must devote to your business to have any chance for success.
- Determine the impact of stepping away from the business for a certain period of time and what steps you would need to become re-engaged with potential clients.
- Determine how you decide if your business is succeeding or if you need to close up shop? What will be the timing of that decision?
- Outline your back-up plan if your business fails.

CHAPTER 15

Family Dynamics

Family is not an important thing. It's everything.

—Michael J. Fox

All happy families resemble one another; each unhappy family is unhappy in its own way.

—Leo Tolstoy

Although placed at the end, this is one of the most important chapters of this book. Being a solopreneur allows you more time with your family, but it also puts certain burdens on your family.

In preparing to write this book, I asked my wife to look back and think about what she liked most about my consulting business and what she liked the least. Her positive comments all related to the flexibility the job provided and how I was able to be there for the kid's events as well as when any minor (or major) emergency arose.

Her dislikes were a much longer list, including no steady income, her concerns about customers failing to pay me for work done, my time spent (wasted?) at unproductive networking events, and the amount of travel required.

Show Me the Money

Money, or more precisely the lack of it, can lead to many heated family discussions if you are not careful. The loss of a regular paycheck is a big change for many people. As the business owner, consultant, and chief bottle washer, you have visibility into your pipeline. Your family does not. I generally know my income projections for the next several months. My wife just sees the balance and deposits in the checkbook. Inevitably, one-person businesses experience ebbs and flows in the business income. You need to understand how that impacts your personal cash management.

Your family is not always aware of future potential business and cannot see a pipeline of potential revenue. They may not understand your market or even truly understand the services you offer. It is incumbent upon you to get your family on board and let them know ahead of time when business is looking slow. You need to communicate a solid plan to be able to weather the ups and downs your business encounters.

If you do not expect to have any significant income for 6 to 12 months when first starting a business, your family better damn well be on board for that trip. If not, trouble is only months away. Even once your business is up and going, there will be low spots in your income or cashflow, if only for a month or two. I want to emphasize again the importance of communication with your spouse regarding your plan, what you see happening in the future, and his or her expectations.

Fortunately, my wife was understanding about our income during my start-up days, but, to this day, never lets me forget about the customer who never paid his bill. (In part, that was due to me buying and paying for his product without him completely paying for my services.) She still worries other clients will stiff me. Bottom line, you need to talk openly and frequently with your significant other about your income and future revenues.

Time

Time is an interesting issue. The premise of a solopreneur business is to spend more time with your family and doing the things you like. But, operating a real business still takes a significant time commitment.

When working for a company, I was usually in the office before 8:00 am and would leave work between 5:30 and 6:00 pm. I would occasionally be in the office Saturday mornings. My vacations usually let me get completely away from the office for at least a brief period.

Now my schedule is as varied as the calendar. On certain days, I have no billable client work at all and I need to be focused on my marketing and sales efforts. I need to constantly evaluate all of the available day time and evening networking opportunities and take advantage of them when possible. Some days, I need to drive several hours to reach my client, leaving by 6:00 in the morning and not returning until after 8:00 in the evening. That is what is necessary to keep the client happy.

The trade-off is that I can schedule to take time off whenever I want to (barring some unique client requirement) but I end up thinking about my business even while I am on vacations. My eldest son recently got married, and for each of the two weeks preceding the ceremony, I was traveling out of town to satisfy a customer requirement. The customer work simply could not be rescheduled, but that did not make it any easier on those planning the wedding and counting on my being there to help.

One of the toughest challenges for your family is the situation where you are now physically closer to family members while you work (working from home), but are *not available* to them because you are buried in your work. Boundaries need to be set. Your family needs to learn to give you the time you need to focus on work knowing they can get your time later to focus on them. Your children might not understand why you cannot play with them when they get home from school midafternoon or even when you have to go to networking events in the evening. Your spouse might not understand why you do not have time to meet with repairmen because you are home anyhow or why you cannot drop everything to help bring in groceries or do other chores around the house during the working day. I let my wife know when I can be available.

While working at home, non-billable time is still a part of your work day. You need to invest time in office work, marketing, networking, and planning your business activities.

Emotional Support

Unless you thrive on adversity, you need to believe in yourself and your spouse needs to believe in you as well. You need to have the backing of your immediate family. If your spouse sees your business only as your response to a mid-life crisis, you have trouble. You need the dual commitment. As a solopreneur, your spouse plays a vital role even if only as a sounding board. That does not mean you agree on every business decision, but you should certainly be talking about any significant ones. Discuss what is best for your entire family unit.

No man (or woman) is an island. It just feels that way from time to time for a one-person business. Your family needs to be there to support you through the rough patches and to help celebrate your wins and achievements. They also provide a connection to the outside world. I have been immersed for days in large computer-based projects where it was wonderful to be able to put all of that aside for a while to hear what happened to my kids in school that day.

Other lifestyle consultants shared some of their family issues with me:

- Your spouse or significant other may feel pressure to maintain a job they do not like. Their income might be crucial during the startup of your business, and their job may be providing medical insurance for the entire family.
- If you work from home, you need to have a dedicated space where you do your work. Using the kitchen table is not the best idea if it needs to be cleared off before every meal. You want a space where you can concentrate on your work and not be distracted by your kids playing video games or watching television.
- Resentment can build if you are able to enjoy the fruits of a lifestyle business while your spouse is still tied to the *nine-to-five* grind of a regular job. You are the one who sees the kids' events while the spouse has to stay at work.
- Balancing the short-term needs of your customers with the longer-term needs of your family can be a real challenge. Almost everyone prioritizes their families before a customer, but there are times when meeting the needs of the customer trumps all else. Perhaps, they need a report finished by a specific deadline or need a project completed. The balancing act is tricky, but remember, you chose a lifestyle business for a reason. Do not allow yourself to be bullied by your clients. Your business provides more individual flexibility, but you do need to be responsive in meeting your customers' needs.
- Your extended family may have a distorted impression of what you are doing. If your job is really home-based (except for infrequent client meetings or marketing events), does

your family think you are unemployed and just sit around the house all day? Does your family understand the type of work you do? Explaining Web design work to a grandparent is not an easy task. Other generational issues exist as well. Today, the Internet allows much more work to be done at home than was ever possible in the past. Once again, communication, with patience, is your best tool in overcoming your family's misperceptions.

Inc. magazine had an excellent piece titled *8 Tips on Preparing Your Family For Entrepreneurship.*[1] While not addressing a lifestyle business specifically, it is a good read to better understand family issues that arise.

Chapter 15: Homework
- Talk to your significant other. Share your business notebook with them. Perhaps if they read this book, they might better understand the journey you are starting and why you are taking it. They might try harder to talk you out of it!
  - o Communicate on the money issues.
  - o Communicate on the time requirements.
- Collectively celebrate your successes.
  - o If your family is going to suffer the pains of your business, they should certainly be part of the wins as well.

---

[1] http://inc.com/guides/201102/how-to-prepare-your-family-for-entrepreneurship.html

CHAPTER 16

Conclusion

Going out on your own may look glamorous and care free. It can be exactly the opposite.

You need to make sure you have an adequate safety net and be able to logically explain to your family what you are doing. If you are married, your spouse has to buy into this 100 percent. If your parents question you, you need to be able to explain why you will not have to move back into their house in three months.

The more preparation and legwork you do while you are still working in a full-time position, the better. Before cutting the strings, make sure you can easily answer the following questions:

- What is the scope of services you will be offering?
- Who are the customers who will be buying your services?
- What is the size of the market for your services?
- What is the value of your services to the customer?
- How can you explain to others the service and its value in less than two minutes? In 25 words?
- What activities will be required to reach your target market?
- How will you survive for six months with little or no income—assume 25 percent of what you are making today (maybe you have already moved back home)?
- And finally, is your family comfortable with your decision and backing you emotionally?

I hope you have found this book useful. If it has helped even one person in becoming a lifestyle entrepreneur (or even convinces one not to do so), then it has been successful. Every business is different, and I wish all of you the best of success.

I would enjoy hearing of your own personal success and challenges in running a solopreneur consulting practice. Maybe you even have some good resources, tips, or best practices you would be willing to share with me. Please feel free to reach out to me at steve@fieldconsulting.biz starting with the word *Book* in the e-mail subject line.

Final Exam

You can feel comfortable starting your consulting business once you can answer all of the following questions:

1. Have you defined your marketable skill or service?
2. Can you describe your offering in 25 words so that a stranger would understand what you do?
3. Have you made sure there is a large enough market for your offering?
4. Have you created a financial plan outlining your income goals and expenses?
5. Have you created a contingency plan for when your goals deviate from reality?
6. Do you have a good lawyer and accountant who can help you when necessary?
7. Have you determined how you are going to market your skills or services?
8. Have you created a list of potential clients with at least 50 names?
9. Do you have adequate insurance coverage?
10. Do you have the personality to accept rejection, exceed your client's expectations, and behave in a professional and ethical manner?

Bonus Question—You must get this one right!

Have you had a good conversation with others in your family that will be impacted by your decision to start a business, discussing your answers to these 10 questions?

Author's Notes

My dad was an excellent father and mentor for me. He was a successful lawyer and provider for our family. He was always available to talk about business or personal issues. We had a wonderful life growing up and were able to enjoy significant family time on vacations or at our lake house. The downside was he worked very hard, had to travel for business, and was rarely able to watch the school events or other day-to-day activities in which I or my brothers participated.

I got married later in life than many of my peers. The birth of my second son was a time for reflection on the importance of my family. About the same time, the company I worked for, Irwin Magnetics, had been acquired and was moving production overseas. This left me looking for new opportunities, and I investigated the potential of working at a large consulting firm. I remember talking to one firm who told me my first assignment would be in Boston for a month. Next, I would be in Dallas for at least two months, and future work locations and travel would be determined when the time came. Yikes!

I decided I wanted to be a larger part of my children's life while they were growing up and was willing to make certain career and financial concessions to allow this to happen. This was a lifestyle decision. Fortunately, after being laid off from Irwin Magnetics on a Friday, I was asked to return to the company as a consultant the following Monday. That was the start of my consulting career.

Both of my boys participated in a variety of sports (soccer, basketball, tennis) and theater activities. I do not claim that every school singing event was a rousing musical success, but I was there. I am almost positive I never missed a high-school home game or show and attended many away matches as well. Frequently, I arranged my consulting business meetings to happen on a specific day, time, and place so that I would finish the day attending an away game in that city.

Both boys ended up winning High School State championships in tennis, one in singles and one in doubles. I was there to cheer them on and witness their success. That was only going to happen once in their lives, and I got to share it with them.

Most evening our family would have dinner together lovingly prepared by my wife. My rule of thumb was to find clients I could drive to during the day, do my consulting work, and be home in time for dinner. This gave us a chance to bond as a family and to hear how everyone's day had been.

We took family vacations, maybe not as extravagant as I had as a child, but nice ones, nonetheless.

This was the lifestyle I chose. My boys are now adults and out on their own, but I do not regret one minute of the time I was able to spend watching them grow up.

Appendix 1

Book List and Other References (in Date Sequence)

—*Hello and a Handshake* by Greg Peters, 2017

—*The Irresistible Consultant's Guide to Winning Clients* by David A. Fields, 2017

—*Home Business Tax Deductions* by Stephen Fishman, J. D., 2017 (look for the latest version)

—*The Only Investment Guide You'll Ever Need* by Andrew Tobias, 2016

—*Guide to Starting and Operating a Small Business,* MI-SBDC, 2015
   http://sbdcmichigan.org/guidetostarting/

—*The One Thing* by Gary Keller and Jay Papasan, 2013

—*One Person/Multiple Careers: A New Model for Work/Life Success* by Marci Alboher, 2012

—*The Education of Millionaires* by Michael Ellsberg, 2012

—*The Startup of You* by Reid Hoffman and Ben Casnocha, 2012

—*Built to Sell* by John Warrillow, 2011

—*Start with Why* by Simon Sinek, 2009
   https://google.com/search?q=simon+sinek+ted+talk+youtube
   &oq=Simon+snek+Ted+Talk&aqs=hrome.2.69i57j0l5.12798
   j0j7&sourceid=chrome&ie=UTF-8

—*The 29% Solution* by Ivan Misner, 2008

—*Field Guide to Consulting and Organizational Development* by Carter McNamara, 2006
   Much of the content from this book can be found at http://man-agementhelp.org/staffing/consulting.htm#anchor264842

—*Endless Referrals* by Bob Burg, 2006

—*Little Black Book of Connections* by Jeffrey Gitmer, 2006

—*The 22 Immutable laws of Branding* by Al Ries and Jack Trout, 2002

—*Spare Room Tycoon* by James Chan, 2000

—*Achieving Success Through Social Capital* by Wayne Baker, 2000

—*Swim with the Sharks Without Being Eaten Alive* by Harvey B. Mackay, 1988

Appendix 2

Subcontractor Agreement

This agreement dated September 1, 20XX, is between Field Consulting Services, LLC, Ann Arbor, MI, and ABC Consulting located in Cleveland, OH.

Scope of Services and Consideration

The subcontractor will provide quality consulting, training, and implementation services and will deliver these services to the FCS clients on a project-by-project basis at the client's designated site. FCS will approve project or training plans prior to the start of work.

FCS agrees to pay the subcontractor a daily or hourly rate of $XXX/hour plus travel expenses for days to be determined. Each new project will be evaluated for daily rate and other consideration prior to beginning work on the project.

There is no compensation for travel time. Actual and reasonable travel expenses and fees earned are to be itemized and submitted to FCS. Travel expenses must be itemized on an expense report form along with appropriate receipts. If you do not have an expense report form, FCS will provide one for you. Receipts are required for any item that exceeds $20.00 (USD). See Attachment A for guidelines on reasonable travel expense.

Representation

FCS was established to provide high-quality consulting, training, and implementation services. In an effort to support this philosophy, it is important that the subcontractor not engage in direct marketing or discussions, which are not supportive of the project's business goals.

Additionally, the subcontractor agrees not to make any representations regarding FCS products or services that are inaccurate or misleading.

Leads for additional support, be it consulting, training, or implementation services resulting directly from work on FCS projects are to be referred to FCS. Direct leads include requests for services resulting from participation in FCS projects, either during or after the timeframe of a project, and information related to potential client plans gained during the timeframe of a project that could lead to future work.

In addition, the subcontractor further agrees that he or she shall not contract with any FCS client with whom he or she has become involved with during the performance of this agreement for a period of no less than one year following the completion of his or her involvement with that client. The date of completion shall be the date of the final check issued to the subcontractor for the services rendered to that client.

Independent Contractor Limitations

It is understood that by providing services, the subcontractor is acting as an independent contractor and not as an employee of FCS. It is recognized that an independent contractor may be undertaking assignments for others. If there is reason to believe that there may be a conflict of interest between the subcontractor's interests and FCS' interests, then the subcontractor will discuss with appropriate management staff of FCS, activities with such other clients to determine the possibility of a conflict of interest. It is understood further that the subcontractor agrees to keep in strictest confidence all matters and materials that are made available to the subcontractor and denoted as "CONFIDEN-TIAL" or which can be reasonably interpreted as being of a sensitive or confidential nature.

Inasmuch as the subcontractor will function as an independent contractor, he or she will not have the status of an employee of FCS, and therefore, will not be eligible for any employee benefits from FCS. FCS will not take any deductions from the subcontractor's fees, either for federal, state, or local tax purposes. It is agreed that the subcontractor shall be solely responsible for his or her own federal, state, and local employment-related taxes and benefits.

Applicable Laws

Michigan laws shall govern this agreement and venue shall be in Washtenaw County.

Assignability

FCS expects the subcontractor to perform services under this agreement. The subcontractor may also supply personnel to the contractor for projects and must ensure that any third party agrees to all obligations under this agreement.

Hold Harmless—No Liability

Subcontractor agrees to hold FCS and its clients harmless from and against all claims, losses, damages, costs, expenses, and reasonable attorney fees related to injury or death to any person, or damage to any property resulting from or arising in connection with the services the subcontractor performs under this agreement, except any injury or property damage resulting from the sole negligence of FCS or its client.

Payments

FCS will invoice clients monthly based on the time and expenses reported by the subcontractor. The subcontractor will be paid once money has been received from the client for that invoice.

FCS will make every reasonable effort to collect money owed by the client in a timely manner.

Terms

Either party may terminate this agreement 30 days after written notice is delivered to the other party. Each party shall be responsible for performing obligations incurred prior to the date of termination.

If these conditions are acceptable to you, please sign and date this copy and return it to FCS at your earliest convenience.

Accepted by:	
For FCS:	For the Subcontractor:
Stephen Field	Name _____
President	Title_____
Field Consulting Services, LLC	Company_____
123 Main Street	Address_____
Ann Arbor, MI 48105	_____
	Phone No. _____
	E-mail_____
Date _____	Date _____
	_____
	Federal ID# or Social Security Number ****

(**** You need to collect your subcontractors' tax IDs and addresses so that you can send them a 1099-MISC form at year end if they do more than $600 of work for you during the calendar year. This is an IRS requirement.)

Subcontractor Agreement—Attachment A

Travel Expense Guidelines

Air Travel

Air travel will be coach class only.

Lodging

Accommodation will be booked at mid-grade hotels or motels such as Quality Inn or Ramada Inn. A separate room for each consultant will be reserved.

Rental Car

Rental cars will be the mid-grade size such as a Ford Taurus class.

Meals

Expenses for meals are expected to be less than $50 per day. Meals will be reimbursed only for days that include an overnight stay.

Personal Auto Mileage

Consultants will be reimbursed for travel to and from an airport or client's site. Personal auto travel is often the preferred method for sites that are located within 250 miles. Miles will be reimbursed at the rate established by the U.S. Government.

Miscellaneous

Parking, tolls, taxis, and tips for baggage handlers will be reimbursed. Receipts for parking and tolls are expected.

FCS must approve any items not included in the above list before expenditures are made. Unapproved expenses may not be reimbursed.

Entertainment and meals purchased for the client are not authorized and will not be reimbursed unless approved prior to the engagement.

Appendix 3

Non-Disclosure Agreement

This agreement dated September 1, 20XX, is between Field Consulting Services, LLC, Ann Arbor, MI, and ABC Consulting located in Cleveland, OH.

In the course of discussions, both parties are likely to or will obtain knowledge of each other's services, trade secrets, and confidential business information. Both parties enter into this Agreement to protect themselves from disclosure of services, trade secrets, and confidential business information to anyone not authorized to obtain the information.

In consideration of premises and agreements hereinafter set forth, Field Consulting Services and ABC Consulting hereby agree as follows:

1. Definition of Confidential Information
For purposes of this Agreement, the term "Confidential Information" shall mean all materials and information related to or associated with either party's services or products, business, or activities, including, but not limited to, trade secrets, product research and development, marketing plans or techniques, reports, client lists, computer data, documentation processes, know-how (whether or not reduced to writing and whether or not patentable or copyrightable), and any non-public financial statements, reports, or information, that:

(a) either party obtains access to or possession of knowledge of, in whole or in part, as a direct or indirect result of discussions, use or inspection of facilities, purchase of services and resources, or otherwise; and

(b) are not part of the public domain at the time of disclosure. However, this Agreement shall not apply to any Confidential Information when and if it subsequently becomes part of the public domain through no action or inaction of either party.

Failure to mark any such Confidential Information as "Confidential" shall not affect its status as Confidential Information within the meaning of this Paragraph 1.

2. Non-Disclosure of Confidential Information

At all times during the term of the consulting engagement, and for three years thereafter, both parties shall hold the Confidential Information in strictest secrecy and shall not directly or indirectly copy, reproduce, manufacture, duplicate, reveal, report, publish, disclose, cause to be disclosed, or transfer any of the Confidential Information to any person or entity, or utilize any Confidential Information for any purpose whatsoever other than as authorized in writing by both parties.

3. Construction

Both parties agree to protect each other from the loss of the proprietary status of any and all Confidential Information, and accordingly agree to safeguard the same in the same manner each party employs for their own trade secrets, but in no event shall either party exercise less than due care and diligence in accordance with Michigan law, U.S. Federal law, good commercial practice, local law, or international law, in whichever affords the highest or best degree of protection.

In witness whereof, the parties have executed this Agreement the date first written above.

for Field Consulting Services, LLC   for ABC Consulting

By: Stephen Field   By:_____
Title: President   Title:_____

Appendix 4A

Terms and Conditions: FCS Example

Billing Practices

Invoices will be issued monthly for hourly work and expenses.

Invoices will be issued as work is completed for project milestone-based work.

Billing rates do not include travel expense, which will be billed separately.

Travel time to and from the customer site in excess of two hours will be billed to the customer at 50 percent of the contracted hourly rate.

Customer is responsible for any other pre-approved expenses as incurred by FCS, including international phone call, production and procurement of training materials, and so on.

Travel and Living Costs

In addition to professional service fees, the customer is responsible for travel and living expenses as incurred by FCS. If incurred, the following expenses will be billed:

- Business or economy class airfare, hotels, rental vehicles.
- Personal vehicle mileage at the current IRS allowable rate per mile.
- Per diem typically $60/day (for meals and incidental expenses).
- Long-distance telephone, fax, or postage charges.
- Other expenses as mutually agreed in advance directly attributable to the project.

Changes to Professional Fees

FCS reserves the right to modify its rates for professional services upon 30 days prior written notice to the customer after completion of the customer's current project.

Payment Terms

All invoices are payable upon receipt.

Independent Contractor

In the performance of this agreement, FCS and its personnel shall act solely as independent contractors, and no personnel, employees, or agents of FCS shall be deemed to be an employee of the customer. Further nothing in this agreement is to be construed or implied to create a relationship of partners, agency, or joint adventures, or of employer and employee. FCS and its personnel shall not represent themselves as agents of the customer, as authorized to assume or create any obligation of any kind, express or implied, on behalf of the customer or otherwise bind the customer in any manner whatsoever. FCS and its personnel understand that the customer has no obligation under state or federal laws or the laws of any other country regarding employee liability, and the total commitment and liability of the customer in regard to this agreement are limited to the payment of the project fees and expenses as set forth herein.

Confidential Information

All client information of any nature, including client lists, potential sales leads, marketing programs, program objectives, cards, tapes, disks, other media, processes, policies, procedures, work instructions, program code and subroutines, accounting procedures, IT security protection techniques, reports made available by the client to FCS or that may become available to FCS by virtue of this engagement or the relationship created by this engagement shall be held in strict confidence by FCS.

Limited Warranty and Disclaimer

The reporting output from FCS enables clients to compare different solutions and approaches comprehensively for their software needs. FCS expressly disclaims any warranty, EXPRESS OR IMPLIED, including, but not limited to, any implied warranty of merchantability or implied warranty of fitness with regard to the applicability of any software package for the requirements of a given end-user. Liability of FCS is limited to the total fee paid to FCS. FCS shall not be liable for any incidental or consequential damages arising out of or in any way related to the use of this research and reporting.

Litigation on Professional Liability

The client agrees to limit any and all liability for damages, costs of defense, or expenses to be levied against FCS on account of any error, omission, or professional negligence to a sum not to exceed the amount of the fee paid to FCS. In no event shall FCS be liable for any consequential damages, incidental damages, damage for loss of use of property, or damages for loss of profits for any delay or failure in performance not otherwise excluded under this paragraph.

Governing Law

This agreement shall be governed and construed in accordance with the laws of the State of Michigan. The venue for any action brought under or in conjunction with this agreement shall be in Washtenaw County, Michigan. (This should obviously be changed to *your* local county and state.)

Appendix 4B

Terms and Conditions: Third-Party Example

Services

ABC Corporation ("Consultant") will provide consulting and other professional services on behalf of Client as provided in the Scope of Work. Client is defined in the attached Proposal or Scope of Work. Unless otherwise stated, Consultant's Proposal to perform the Scope of Work expires 60 days from its date and may be modified or withdrawn by Consultant prior to receipt of Client's acceptance. The offer and acceptance of any services or goods covered by the Proposal is conditioned upon these terms and conditions. Any additional or different terms and conditions proposed by Client are objected to and will not be binding upon Consultant unless specifically agreed to in writing by Consultant. An order or statement of intent to purchase Consultant's services, or any direction to proceed with, or acquiescence in the commencement of work shall constitute consent to these terms and conditions.

Compensation

Consultant will invoice for their services on a time and materials basis using the Schedule of Rates embodied in the referenced Proposal. Prices or rates quoted do not include state or local taxes where applicable. Services may include reimbursable expenses, which are charges incurred for travel, transportation, temporary lodging, meals, telephone calls, fax, postage, courier service, photographic, photocopying, and other fees and costs reasonably incurred in connection with the services.

Unless otherwise stated in the Proposal, Consultant will submit invoices for services related to the Scope of Work on at least a monthly basis, and Client will make payment within 30 days of receipt of Consultant's invoices. If Client objects to any portion of an invoice, the Client will notify Consultant within 15 days from the date of receipt of the invoice and will pay that portion of the invoice not in dispute, and the parties shall immediately make every effort to settle the disputed portion of the invoice.

If Client fails to make any payment due to Consultant within 30 days after receipt of an invoice, then the amount due to Consultant will increase at the rate of 1.5 percent per month after the 30th day. If a retainer has been required and the Client has not paid the invoice within 30 days, the Consultant shall be entitled to draw upon the retainer to satisfy the past due invoice. In addition, Consultant may, after giving seven days' written notice to Client, suspend its services and any deliverables until Consultant has been paid in full for all amounts outstanding more than 30 days. In the event that Consultant must resort to legal action to enforce collection of payments due, Client agrees to pay attorney fees and any other costs resulting from such action.

Client's Responsibilities

Client will designate in writing the person or persons with authority to act on Client's behalf on all matters concerning the work to be performed by Consultant for Client.

Client will furnish to Consultant all existing studies, reports, data, and other information available to Client, which may be necessary for performance of the work, authorize Consultant to obtain additional data as required, and furnish the services of others, where necessary, for the performance of the work. Consultant will be entitled to use and rely upon all such information and services.

Unless otherwise stated in the Proposal, Client shall be responsible to provide Consultant access to the work site or property to perform the work.

Performance of Service

Consultant's services will be performed in conformance with the Scope of Work set forth in the Proposal.

Additional services will be performed and completed in conformance with any supplemental proposals or Scopes of Work approved in writing by the Client.

Consultant's services for the Scope of Work will be considered complete at the earlier of (i) the date when Consultant's report is accepted by the Client or (ii) 30 days after the date when Consultant's report is submitted for final acceptance, if Consultant is not notified in writing within such 30-day period of a material defect in such report.

If any time period within or date by which any of Consultant's services are to be performed is exceeded for reasons outside of Consultant's reasonable control, all rates, measures and amounts of compensation and the time for completion of performance shall be subject to equitable adjustment.

Confidentiality

Consultant will hold confidential all information obtained from Client, not otherwise previously known to us, unless such information comes into the public domain through no fault of ours, is furnished to us by a third party who is under no obligation to keep such information confidential, or is independently developed by us.

Warranty

In performing services, Consultant agrees to exercise professional judgment, made on the basis of the information available to Consultant, and to use the same standard of care and skill ordinarily exercised in similar circumstances by consultants performing comparable services in the region. This standard of care shall be judged as of the time and place the services are rendered, and not according to later standards. The expiration date of this warranty is one year from the date of completion of the service. Reasonable people may disagree on matters involving professional judgment and, accordingly, a difference of opinion on a question of professional judgment shall not excuse Client from paying for services rendered or result in liability to Consultant.

If any failure to meet the foregoing warranty appears during one year from the date of completion of the service and Consultant is promptly notified thereof in writing, Consultant will, at its option and expense, re-perform the nonconforming work or refund the amount of compensation paid to Consultant for such nonconforming work. In no event shall Consultant be required to bear the cost of gaining access in order to perform its warranty obligations.

THE FOREGOING WARRANTY IS EXCLUSIVE AND IN LIEU OF ALL OTHER WARRANTIES, WHETHER WRITTEN, ORAL, IMPLIED, OR STATUTORY, INCLUDING ANY WARRANTY OF MERCHANTABILITY. CONSULTANT DOES NOT WARRANT ANY PRODUCTS OR SERVICES OF OTHERS DESIGNATED BY CLIENT.

Insurance

Consultant will procure and maintain insurance as required by law. At a minimum, Consultant will have the following coverage:

(a) Worker's compensation and occupational disease insurance in statutory amounts.
(b) Employer's liability insurance in the amount of $1,000,000.
(c) Automotive liability in the amount of $1,000,000.
(d) Comprehensive General Liability insurance for bodily injury, death, or loss of or damage to property of third persons in the amount of $1,000,000 per occurrence, $2,000,000 in the aggregate.
(e) Professional errors and omissions insurance in the amount of $1,000,000.

Indemnity

Each Party will indemnify the other Party, its employees, representatives, contractors, consultants, and agents from and against any claims, costs, liabilities or expenses, including reasonable attorney's fees, to the extent caused by the negligent, reckless, or willful acts of the indemnifying Party in connection with the services hereunder.

Notwithstanding the foregoing, in the event that Consultant performs intrusive ground work as part of the Scope of Work, Client shall indemnify Consultant from and against any and all claims, costs, liabilities, or expenses, including reasonable attorney's fees, resulting from, or arising out of, damages to subsurface or underground utilities or structures, including, but not limited to, gas, telephone, electric, water or sewer utilities whose locations were not designated or identified to Consultant prior to the commencement of any subsurface investigation or cleanup, including, but not limited to, excavation, drilling, boring, or probing required to be conducted by Consultant as part of site investigation, characterization or remediation work.

To the extent the Scope of Work or any Request for Services under this Agreement requires Consultant to communicate (e.g., perform interviews) with any third party including, but not limited to, owners of off-site locations, former employees, current employees or governmental authorities, Consultant shall so inform Client. Client will indemnify Consultant from and claims, costs, liabilities, or expenses, including reasonable attorney's fees to the extent arising from claims of breach of confidentiality, waiver of privilege, or otherwise associated with any such communications.

Allocation of Responsibility

Consultant shall be liable to Client only for direct damages to the extent caused by Consultant's negligence or willful misconduct in the performance of its services. UNDER NO CIRCUMSTANCES SHALL CONSULTANT BE LIABLE FOR INDIRECT, CONSEQUENTIAL, SPECIAL OR EXEMPLARY DAMAGES, OR FOR DAMAGES CAUSED BY CLIENT'S FAILURE TO PERFORM ITS OBLIGATIONS. To the fullest extent permitted by law, the total liability in the aggregate of Consultant and its employees, subcontractors or suppliers to Client and anyone claiming by, through or under Client on all claims of any kind (excluding claims for death or bodily injury) arising out of or in any way related to Consultant's services, or from any cause or causes whatsoever, including, but not limited to, negligence, errors, omissions, strict liability, indemnity, or breach of contract, shall not exceed the total compensation received by Consultant under this agreement, or the total amount of $50,000, whichever is greater. All such liability shall terminate on the expiration date of the warranty period specified in Section 6.

If Consultant furnishes Client with advice or assistance concerning any products, systems, or services, which is not required under the Scope of Work or any other contract among the parties, the furnishing of such advice or assistance will not subject Consultant to any liability whether in contract, indemnity, warranty, tort (including negligence), strict liability, or otherwise.

Disposal of Contaminated Material

Client understands and agrees that Consultant is not, and has no responsibility as, a generator, operator, owner, treater, arranger, or storer of pre-existing substances or wastes found or identified at work sites, including drilling and cutting fluids and other samples. Consultant shall not directly or indirectly assume title to such substances or wastes and shall not be liable to third parties alleging that Consultant has or had title to such materials. Client will indemnify and hold harmless Consultant from and against all losses, damages, costs, and expenses, including, but not limited to, attorneys' fees, arising or resulting from actions brought by third parties alleging or identifying Consultant as a generator, operator, arranger, storer, treater, or owner of pre-existing substances or wastes found or identified at work sites.

Ownership of all samples obtained by Consultant from the project site is maintained by Client. Consultant will store such samples in a professional manner for the period of time necessary to complete the project. Upon completion of the project, Consultant will return any unused samples or portions thereof to Client or, at Consultant's option using a manifest signed by Client as generator, dispose of the samples in a lawful manner, and bill Client for all costs related thereto. Consultant will normally store samples for 30 days.

Ownership of Documents

All notes, memoranda, drawings, designs, specifications, and reports prepared by Consultant shall become Client's upon completion of the payment to Consultant as provided herein.

All documents, including drawings and specifications, prepared by Consultant pursuant to the Scope of Work are instruments of service with respect to this project. Such documents are not intended or represented to be suitable for reuse by Client or by any other party on subsequent extensions or phases of this project or site or on any other project or site without the written consent of both Client and Consultant.

Any reuse without written approval or adaptation by Consultant for the specific purpose intended will be at the Client's sole risk and without liability or legal exposure to Consultant. Any such reuse requested by Client will entitle Consultant to further compensation at rates to be agreed upon by Client and Consultant. A request by Client to provide a letter of reliance to a third party will entitle Consultant to assess a small charge in connection with documenting its consent.

Consultant will retain the technical project file for a period of six years from project completion (if Client is a governmental entity, files shall be maintained for a 10-year period following project completion). Client shall notify Consultant at the completion of work if Client requires the file in this matter to be transferred to Client or another entity, or retained by Consultant for a longer period of time. In the absence of any written instructions to the contrary from Client, Consultant will have the right to discard any and all files, records, or documents of any type related to the Scope of Work after the six-year period. During this six-year period, any requests for document recovery and reproduction will be assessed a fee in accordance with Consultant's Schedule of Fees.

Independent Contractor

Consultant is an independent contractor and shall not be regarded as an employee or agent of the Client.

Compliance with Federal, State, and Local Laws

The Consultant shall observe all applicable provisions of the federal, state, and local laws and regulations, including those relating to equal opportunity employment.

Safety

Client shall be obligated to inform Consultant and its employees of any applicable site safety procedures and regulations known to Client as well as any special safety concerns or dangerous conditions at the site. Consultant and its employees will be obligated to adhere to such procedures and regulations once notice has been given.

Unless specifically provided in the Scope of Work, Consultant shall not have any responsibility for overall job safety at the site. If in Consultant's opinion, its field personnel are unable to access required locations or perform required services in conformance with applicable safety standards, Consultant may immediately suspend performance until such safety standards can be attained. If within a reasonable time site operations or conditions are not brought into compliance with such safety standards, Consultant may, in its discretion, terminate its performance in accordance with Section 17.0, in which event Client shall pay for services and termination expenses as provided herein.

Litigation

At the request of Client, Consultant agrees to provide testimony and other evidence in any litigation, hearings or proceedings to which Client is or becomes a party in connection with the Scope of Work. Client agrees to compensate Consultant at its Litigation Rates in effect at the time the services are rendered for its time and other costs in connection with such evidence or testimony. Similarly, if Consultant is compelled by legal process to provide testimony or produce documents or other evidence in connection with work performed, Consultant agrees to contact Client and cooperate with Client and Client's counsel. Client agrees to compensate Consultant at its Litigation Rates in effect at the time the services are rendered for its time, expense, and retention of counsel in connection with such testimony or document and other evidentiary production.

Notice

All notices to either Party by the other shall be deemed to have been sufficiently given when made in writing and delivered in person, by facsimile, e-mail, certified mail, or courier to the address of the respective Party or to such other address as such Party may designate.

Termination

The performance of work may be terminated or suspended by either Party, in whole or in part. Such termination shall be affected by delivery of seven days prior written notice specifying the extent to which performance of work is terminated and the date upon which such action shall become effective. In the event work is terminated or suspended by Client (or by Consultant as provided herein) prior to the completion of services contemplated hereunder, Consultant shall be paid for (i) the services rendered to the date of termination or suspension; (ii) demobilization costs; (iii) costs incurred with respect to noncancelable commitments; and (iv) reasonable services provided to effectuate a professional and timely project termination or suspension.

Severability

If any term, covenant, condition, or provision of these Terms and Conditions is found by a court of competent jurisdiction to be invalid, void, or unenforceable, the remainder of these Terms and Conditions shall remain in full force and effect, and shall in no way be affected, impaired, or invalidated thereby.

Waiver

Any waiver by either Party or any provision or condition of these Terms and Conditions shall not be construed or deemed to be a waiver of a subsequent breach of the same provision or condition, unless such waiver is so expressed in writing and signed by the Party to be bound.

Governing Law

These Terms and Conditions will be governed by and construed and interpreted in accordance with the laws of the State of Connecticut.

Captions

The captions of these Terms and Conditions are intended solely for the convenience of reference and shall not define, limit, or affect in any way the provisions, Terms and Conditions hereof or their interpretation.

Entire Agreement

These Terms and Conditions, and the Scope of Work, represent the entire understanding and agreement between the parties and supersede any and all prior agreements, whether written or oral, and may be amended or modified only by a written amendment signed by both parties.

About the Author

Stephen D. Field is the President of Field Consulting Services, LLC and has over 30 years of hands-on management and consulting experience in both for-profit and non-profit environments. After starting his career working for large manufacturing corporations and serving in several mid-management and general manager positions, Mr. Field transitioned into the consulting arena. He has a proven track record of delivering executive-level consulting to manufacturing organizations in the areas of operational and financial management, information technology, inventory and production control. Mr. Field has helped over a hundred companies select, install, and better utilize a variety of enterprise business software (ERP) systems. Mr. Field's ability to leverage his deep system's expertise, cross-functional understanding, and focus on results has yielded millions of dollars of benefits to his clients' bottom line. He has written several articles and presented at various trade association conferences across the United States. Mr. Field received his Bachelors of Science in Industrial Engineering at Northwestern University and his MBA from the University of Michigan.

Index

OTHER TITLES IN THE ENTREPRENEURSHIP AND SMALL BUSINESS MANAGEMENT COLLECTION

Scott Shane, Case Western University, Editors

- *Growth-Oriented Entrepreneurship* by Alan S. Gutterman
- *Startup Strategy Humor* by Rajesh K. Pillania
- *The Leadership Development Journey* by Jen Vuhuong
- *Getting to Market With Your MVP* by J.C. Baker
- *From Vision to Decision* by Dana K. Dwyer
- *The Entrepreneurial Adventure* by David James

Announcing the Business Expert Press Digital Library

Concise e-books business students need for classroom and research

This book can also be purchased in an e-book collection by your library as

- a one-time purchase,
- that is owned forever,
- allows for simultaneous readers,
- has no restrictions on printing, and
- can be downloaded as PDFs from within the library community.

Our digital library collections are a great solution to beat the rising cost of textbooks. E-books can be loaded into their course management systems or onto students' e-book readers.
The **Business Expert Press** digital libraries are very affordable, with no obligation to buy in future years. For more information, please visit **www.businessexpertpress.com/librarians**. To set up a trial in the United States, please email **sales@businessexpertpress.com**.